The Kingdom and the Glory

Meditation and Commentary on the Gospel of Matthew

The Kingdom and the Glory

Meditation and Commentary on the Gospel of Matthew

Alfred McBride, O. Praem.

Our Sunday Visitor Publishing Division
Our Sunday Visitor, Inc.
Huntington, Indiana 46750

Nihil Obstat: Reverend Richard J. Murphy, O.M.I.
                 Censor Deputatus

Imprimatur: Reverend Msgr. William J. Kane, V.G.
                 Vicar General for the Archdiocese of Washington
                 July 16, 1991

The nihil obstat and imprimatur are official declarations that a book or pamphlet is free of doctrinal or moral error. No implication is contained therein that those who have granted the nihil obstat and the imprimatur agree with the content, opinions or statements expressed.

ISBN: 0-87973-355-1
LCCCN: 91-62161

PRINTED IN THE UNITED STATES OF AMERICA

Cover design by Rebecca J. Heaston
Editorial production by Kelley L. Renz
355

Dedicated to Jack Taylor who conceived this project of New Testament commentaries, encouraged me to go ahead, and developed the start-up support.

Contents

Foreword

On the road to Emmaus, Jesus gave his two friends a Scripture lesson. He took the Bible as though it were a loaf of bread and broke it open to feed their hearts, minds, feelings, and souls. He explained how the prophets, wisdom speakers, psalm singers, storytellers, and patriarchs sang and spoke of the essential link between the sufferings of the Messiah and his glory. "Was it not necessary that the Messiah should suffer these things and so enter his glory?" (Lk. 24:26).

Luke does not give us the details of that remarkable Scripture lesson, other than to say the listeners were so moved that their hearts burned within them. Jesus gave them an experience of Scripture that caused a personal spiritual and moral conversion. The Christian interpretation of Scripture ever since has drawn two essential guidelines from that scene. First, all of Scripture illumines the meaning and purpose of Jesus Christ's work of salvation. Second, the biblical words call each of us to a faith conversion to Jesus Christ.

No interpreter of Scripture ever understood these principles better than St. Augustine. For him the soul was the home of all the feelings in the body. Since Christians were members of Christ's Body, they could get in touch with the inner life of Jesus, his soul if you will. As Augustine scanned the pages of Scripture, he found in the psalms the record of the feelings of Jesus. The psalms and the gospels were more than two books written in different periods of history; they were the seamless garment of the love story between God and people, one text illuminating the other.

The Christ of Augustine's sermons on the gospels possesses the quiet majesty of classic art. But in his commentaries on the psalms, Augustine comes upon a flood of emotions and applies them to Jesus. The figure of the passionate King David supplies the vision of the emotions of Jesus. Hence it is Christ's voice that is heard in the psalms, "a voice singing happily, a voice rejoicing in hope, a voice sighing in its present state. We should know his voice, feel it intimately, make it our own" (*Commentary on Psalms*, 42,1).

At the same time, Augustine wanted to do more than stir up feeling in the listeners to his Scripture sermons. He wanted to break bread and feed the multitude. As a boy, he had stolen fruit to share with his comrades. As a bishop, he raided the fields of Scripture to feed his parishioners to whom he ministered for forty years. "I go to feed so I can give you to eat. I lay before you that from which I draw my life" (*Fragments*, 2,4). He was interested in converting his listeners to Jesus ever more deeply through the Scriptures.

He wrote to Jerome that he could never be a disinterested Bible scholar. "If I gain any new knowledge of Scripture, I pay it out immediately to God's people" (*Letter*, 73,2).

Pope John Paul II stressed these same principles about Scripture interpretation in an address to the members of the Biblical Commission. He noted with satisfaction the progress being made in modern Catholic biblical scholarship since the encyclical *Providentissimus* written by Pope Leo XIII in 1893. He cited the many forms of scientific analysis of Scripture which have developed, such as the study of literary forms, semiotics, and narrative analysis.

He dwelt on the "limitations" of the new methods and asked his listeners to avoid the excesses of the swings of fashion in Scripture interpretation, for example, one school totally preoccupied with history and another one forgetting history altogether. He also advised his audience to observe the one-sidedness of some interpreters of Scripture such as those who cite Vatican II's document on Scripture (*Dei Verbum*) in support of the use of scientific methods, but seem to forget the other teaching of the council that interpreters should never forget the divine authorship of the Bible.

His next words deserve to be quoted in full:

The Bible has certainly been written in human language. Its interpretation requires the methodical use of the science of language. But it is also God's Word. Exegesis (Scripture interpretation) would be seriously incomplete if it did not shed light on the theological significance of Scripture.

We must not forget that Christian exegesis is a theological discipline, a deepening of the faith. This entails an interior tension between historical research founded on verifiable facts and research in the spiritual order based on faith in Christ. There is a great temptation to eliminate this inner tension by renouncing one or another of these two orientations . . . to be content with a subjective interpretation which is wrongly called "spiritual," or a scientific interpretation which makes the texts "sterile."

—English Edition of *L'Osservatore Romano*, April 22, 1991

This commentary/meditation which you are about to read was written with this total vision in mind. You will not find it heavily scientific because it was not meant to be a popularization of the scientific methods of interpretation. At the same time, it is meant to reflect the beneficial results of scientific studies. You will discover it is aimed at opening up the person, message, and work of Jesus Christ whose work of salvation in union with the Father and the Holy Spirit is presented. Therefore, Jesus centered and faith growth envisioned.

It is my hope that these reflections will draw you to love the Bible, and in so doing, love Christ, yourself, and others. We are thus loving more than a book or sacred texts, we are in a total love affair. Perhaps Chaim Potok's description of the "Dance of the Torah" has something to say to us here. The scene is a Hasidic Synagogue in the Williamsburg section of Brooklyn. A religious festival is in progress and the participants have reached a part of the ceremony where scrolls of the Torah are passed around and certain privileged members are allowed to dance with it. We pick up the scene as the principal character, who has been agonizing about his faith and its relation to life, is handed the scroll.

I held the scroll as something precious to me, a living being with whose soul I was forever bound, this Sacred Scroll, this Word, this Fire of God, this Source for my own creation, this velvet encased Fountain of All Life which I now clasped in a passionate embrace. I danced with the Torah for a long time, following the line of dancers through the steamy air of the synagogue and out into the chill tumultuous street and back into the synagogue and then reluctantly yielding the scroll to a huge dark-bearded man who hungrily scooped it up and swept away with it in his arms.

—*The Gift of Asher Lev*, paperback, p. 351

Should not our encounter with Scripture be a dance with the Holy Word?

There was an old folk custom, now lost in the mists of history, in which a child was formally introduced to the sweetness of the Word of God. A page of the Bible was given to the child. Upon the page was spread some honey and the child was asked to taste it. Hence from earliest youth, the child would be introduced to a positive experience of Scripture, the sweetness of the Word of God.

What else need be said?

"How sweet are thy words to my taste,
sweeter than honey to my mouth."

—Ps. 119:103, RSV

Introduction

In "A Man for All Seasons" there is a scene that reveals the humanity of Thomas More in an unforgettable way. On the eve of the trial that would condemn him to death, More is visited by Alice, his wife, and family. He notices that Alice looks distant and distressed. He compliments her on the lunch she brought with its "superlative custard." It does not warm her. He praises her new dress. She remains unmoved. He then reaches out to her and, childlike, pleads for her to understand what he is doing. He wants her to understand his conscience dilemma. He must oppose the king's position regarding the pope and the divorce. Alice keeps resisting, partly because she sees the negative impact this has on their family. With tears in his eyes, More hugs her and begs for understanding. He feels he cannot die a proper death without it. Finally, she says that the one thing she does understand is that she is married to the best man she can ever hope to meet. Moreover, she will tell the king himself if need be.

Joyously, More cries out, "Why, it's a lion I married. A lion!" The brilliant former tutor of the king and chancellor of England had the common touch. He was not afraid to show he had a human need.

The gospels, of all the world's literature, possess this same capacity. No matter how often they are read or how numerous the commentaries, they are matchless literature, the people's poetry at its best. Of the four gospels, Matthew's seems closest to the common touch, perhaps because the author was a tax collector, one who, like anyone dealing with financial transactions, observed human expression in one of its perennial sharper forms.

The Kingdom Book

The title of this book reflects the central theme of Matthew, namely the kingdom. Matthew carefully builds the stories and teachings of Jesus around the issue of the kingdom, which is the spiritual dimension of the Christian religion. Recent studies about the meaning of the church have tended to concentrate on this kingdom aspect more than on the church's external organizational form. Such studies have recovered rich religious meanings of the church by shifting the emphasis to the kingdom in order to create a spiritual impact on the members and their witness to the world. It is not a question of opposing kingdom to organization. Both are obviously needed. The interior spiritual kingdom requires a public structure to serve its demands and make public witness a systematic possibility. An organization, however, is a dead branch if there is no interior spirit pushing it to move beyond a preoccupation with self-serving or a morbid sense of siege.

Matthew was able to witness both aspects: the original sense of kingdom in all its spiritual liveliness, and the gradual movements toward an organized church as the new Christians made the normal human effort to structure themselves so that the message of Jesus would be preserved and good order would sustain the life of the members.

But Matthew's Gospel is not an account of the building of the structure. That is to be found in Acts. His is the story of the beginning of the kingdom, the first appearance of the community of believers struggling to grasp the inner mystery that Christ patiently unfolds for them.

In order to bring the meaning of the kingdom alive Matthew weaves together ethics, prophecy, miracles, and parables.

Ethics

Matthew's record of the Sermon on the Mount (Chapters 5-7) spells out the ethical charter of the kingdom. It describes, in a variety of ways, what a kingdom person would be like. It is an ideal picture built out of the covenant style used by Moses at Sinai. There, the charter of the Ten Commandments is followed by the moral ideals of Deuteronomy and the worship ideals of Leviticus. The charter occurs within the glory of Sinai where God pledges his love to Israel. The subsequent ideals are illustrations of that covenant love.

In Matthew the kingdom's charter includes the eight Beatitudes, followed by a long series of moral ideals that flesh out the possibilities of a mature Christian. It may be that only rarely does any individual fulfill all these ideals. The point is that the ideals are known and available for the soul-stretching necessary to grow to fullness in Christ.

Prophecy

Matthew is very fond of quoting the prophets. Some believe he was trying to appeal to his Jewish readers. If they could be persuaded by the logic of the fulfillment texts they might be open to receiving Christ. It is very possible that this was Matthew's intent.

However, he may also be reminding his readers that it was the prophets who kept alive the theme of the kingdom throughout the numerous distractions caused by wicked kings, sinful people, the anguish of exile, the trying circumstances of the return, and the sheer boredom of housekeeping in the ensuing years. Prophets were never completely at home in the external structures of religion produced by the old covenant. It was not that they were against these structures per se; simply, it was their mission to speak for the inner world of the spirit, and they knew well how heavy and blinding external structures can be.

Some critics point out that Matthew stretches the point too often when he correlates prophetic statements with kingdom events in Christ's life. But Matthew is not reaching for logical consistency so much as for a meta-logical message. He is illustrating a spiritual consistency between the prophets and Jesus. It is they who kept alive the small flame that Jesus now ignites into a blazing fire. It is, therefore, important to read the persistent thread of prophetic statements as a joyous *Amen* from those ancients who were so gloriously pleased to see Jesus break into the world's consciousness in an absolute and world-shaking manner.

Miracles

Matthew teaches like a good rabbi. In a rabbinical school typology and argumentation mean a great deal. Typology uses outstanding historical events as types or definitive examples against which all new events are to be measured and interpreted. It is, however, more than the mere matching of old and new histories. The connection is more than external. It is mystical. For example, the greatest event in the history of Israel was the liberation from Egypt and its conclusion in the covenant at Sinai. The significance of any other historical moment is measured against that primordial experience of God. The mystical connection is God's power experienced by the believing people. So, the liberation from Babylon some centuries later, like the ancient freedom event, is seen as an act of God. It is God's loving action in their lives that ties all their history together and gives meaning to what they do.

This method of event-matching in the spiritual framework of God's covenant love is wedded to the rabbinical method of argumentation. Hot debates still regularly occur in the halls of the *yeshiva*, or community school, where the study of the Torah/Bible takes place. Such arguments do not as a rule produce enemies. The Russians have a proverb to explain this: A yes man is your enemy. Your friends will argue with you. The give and take of argument brings the truth to light and makes the Torah relevant for each new age of believers. When the spark of truth inflames the minds of the members of the yeshiva a special psalm of praise arises, for intimacy of God's kingdom touches their hearts.

Much of this system of typology and argument appears in Matthew. We have already noted how the Sermon on the Mount parallels the historical event of the covenant on the mountain of Sinai. To see the difference, we need only note that Luke places the giving of the Beatitudes in a valley, while Matthew places Jesus/New Moses on a mountain. This makes clearer that the new event is an inbreaking of God even greater than Sinai—which would be a revolutionary announcement for Matthew, since normal rabbinical procedure would always say Sinai is the supreme norm. True, they looked for an event greater than Sinai, but it was so long in coming they were reluctant even to note the arrival of the new covenant.

The miracle stories are told within the mood of typological teaching. Just as God wrought marvels against the evil pharaoh to gain freedom for his people, so Christ now performs marvels/miracles against the Prince of Darkness to gain freedom not just for one people, but for the whole world. In the narrative of the ten plagues, God fights against evil on a limited scale for the sake of a single people. In Matthew's narrative of the ten miracles, Jesus fights on a cosmic scale against evil for the sake of every human being for all time.

Allied to the use of typology is the fondness for argumentation as the way to get at the truth. The commentary will dwell on the many places Jesus enters into arguments with the Pharisees, the Sadducees and the priests. In general, these should not be interpreted in the spirit of contentiousness as though the partners to the argument are out to get each other. Jesus and the religious leaders were not polarized at first. He and his fellow arguers were engaged in normal rabbinical give and take. It was only as time went on that it became clear that there was a radical difference between Christ and the others. Jesus, quite simply, was too far ahead of them. His message about the kingdom was too much for them to accept and presented the threat that eventually led some of them to call for his death.

We have become so accustomed to seeing the world-embracing vision of Christianity that we fail to note how revolutionary it was in the beginning and how remarkably powerful was the grace of Christ to stretch the minds of a few provincial fisherman and a crusty rabbinical student, Paul, to give themselves to such an astonishing mission.

There is an additional point about the miracles. This book contains some comments on the interpretation of miracles that would seem to deny their possibility. If the tone is strong in taking issue with this point of view, it is perhaps due to what appears to be an excess of special pleading for the opposite point. Readers should not be derailed by these observations.

Parables

Rabbis excel in event-matching (typology) and debate. They are also enormously competent in storytelling or parable composition. In fact, the story method pervades much of the Middle East. Every school child knows the fables of Aesop. The Tales from the Arabian Nights have inspired numerous musicals, operas and art works.

Matthew records the superb storytelling ability of Jesus in the parables. The appreciation of the parables involves an understanding of the use of language among biblical people. Language reflects thought patterns. In the West the dominant thought pattern is logic. As we well know, this does not mean that all western people are logical. It does mean that logical ways of thinking hold the place of honor. A counterpart of logical thinking is the emphasis on the abstract in preference to the concrete.

Biblical thinking, on the other hand, is concrete and poetic. Instead of abstracting the idea from its concrete base, the biblical thinker will be earthy in the best sense of that word; he will prefer the full image in words. Instead of chains of logic, he works in coils and spools of circular thinking.

How does this work? If a westerner wants to teach the truth that a person will inevitably die, he or she may use a syllogism: All people are mortal. John is a person. Therefore, John is mortal. The biblical thinker will simply tell ten stories about different kinds of people who have died until the listener gets the point that people die.

Such general observations must be modified. Surely there is poetry in western people. One need only recall Shakespeare. Just as certainly, there is logic among biblical thinkers, but it is not so pronounced or abstract as among their western counterparts.

A third element differentiates the westerner from the biblical person. It is the power of language. To the westerner talk is cheap. It is not so with the bible person. Talk is powerful and produces what it says. Biblical words bear a creative and dynamic meaning, a binding power. The closest counterparts in contemporary thinking are court oaths and testimony, and wedding vows.

The reason for this digression into the different forms of thought and language is to emphasize the seriousness of the parables of

Jesus. Storytellers in contemporary society are entertainers and are not usually regarded as serious thinkers. In the Bible the storyteller is taken very seriously and honored as a first-rate thinker. Wisdom and power and meaning emanate from his well-wrought stories.

The parables of Jesus are stories weighted with endless circles of meaning. Two thousand years later they retain the power to charm the mind, provoke curiosity and lure the imagination to new forms of application to contemporary life. In Matthew's Gospel these parables are pointed toward the meaning of the kingdom.

If miracles provide the drama for the establishment of the kingdom, parables offer the evocations of its spiritual mystery. Language to describe it will always be reaching for clarity and honesty of communication. The beauty of the parable/poetry approach is that it contains language with shimmering vibrations, like the resonances of a church bell in an alpine valley. A sense of "more than" (transcendence) is preserved by such language and thus is more successful in making the mystery of the kingdom come alive and inviting the listener to be open to its possibilities.

Infancy Narratives

Matthew opens his gospel with the Christmas story. His emphasis is on the wise men who honor Jesus as the newborn leader of the kingdom. Matthew's account is basically the material for the feast of the Epiphany. It is in Luke that the Christmas-card stories of angels and shepherds, and the inhospitable innkeeper are told.

Passion Narrative

Matthew's extensive account of the passion and resurrection is the one most frequently read, though Luke and John add many details which have become the substance of Christian devotion and art. Bach's musical rendition of the Matthew passion offers a most exalted interpretation of this gospel.

The Commentary

The approach taken in this commentary is meant to be "popular" in the best sense of that word. Scholarly apparatus is avoided though scholarship is not, and every effort is made to use meaningful contemporary language. In no sense is this an exhaustive approach. It is a mixture of cultural observations, devotional meditations, shreds of poetry and occasional fictional dramatization, as in the case of the temptation of Jesus and the famed passage about finding Christ in the neighbor who has needs. Writing a commentary on Matthew's Gospel is more than a technical task of composition. It is a spiritual meditation and a work of faith. The present writer is a more grace-filled man for having so closely lived with the text of Matthew for the better part of a year and hopes that others may come to know and love the kingdom as much as he who wishes to express gratitude to the Lord Jesus for all his marvelous works.

Ave Maria!
O bone Jesu, miserere nobis!

1   Trees and Dreams

Ancestors of Jesus (Mt. 1:1-17)

Royal families specialize in lineage. Matthew begins his story of the King of kings with a family tree. It connects Jesus with the royalty of Israel and clearly is intended to show that he is the Savior, the fulfillment of the promise made to Abraham. Matthew gives us three sets of fourteen names.

Hebrews were fond of assigning a numerical value to a letter. The letters of King David's name totaled fourteen. Thus, the three sets of fourteen names were a way of exultantly saying David three times, a way by which Matthew connected the beloved King David to the royal child of Bethlehem. If the old David could inspire Israel to dreams of hope, how much more will this "thrice-blessed David-Jesus"[*] become the universal hope of the world! Born a king, he will establish the universal kingdom of God.

Although this family tree looks like a male chauvinist's list — Israel was a patriarchal society — four women do occupy prominent branches. Three of them would normally prove embarrassing. Tamar seduced her father-in-law Judah into an incestuous union (Gn. 38). Rahab, chief call girl of Jericho, sheltered Joshua's spies. For her valuable services she was brought into the Israelite community (Jos. 2).

Bathsheba, wife of Uriah, entered into an adulterous union with David and was a willing accomplice in the subsequent murder of her husband (2 Sm. 11-12). Only Ruth, devoted daughter-in-law of Naomi, emerges as a respectable female ancestor of Jesus. All four women were foreigners, though there is some debate about

---

[*]William Neill, comp., *Harper's Bible Commentary* (New York: Harper and Row, 1961), p. 335.

Bathsheba's alien status. Why were they included? Most likely to show that Jesus had gentile forebears. His ecumenical lineage foreshadows the universal extent of his mission and message.

Luke also has a family tree (Lk. 3:23-38). He cites some other ancestors, not mentioned by Matthew, and omits the lists of Kings. Early church fathers loved to debate the two tree lists, but their results were inconclusive. To this day we do not know why the lists are so diverse.

Joseph's Dream (Mt. 1:18-25)

To solve the dilemma presented to Joseph by Mary's pregnancy, the angel appears to him in a dream. Such divine messengers often appear in Old Testament crises. Here, the heavenly counselor reassures Joseph that Mary's pregnancy is the result of the work of the Holy Spirit.

Jewish marriage customs attached a greater importance to the engagement ceremony than does today's western society. In effect, the engagement was the beginning of the marriage companionship, though sexual privileges were deferred until after the actual marriage. Thus, the period between the engagement and the wedding ceremony amounted to a legal limbo.

In this betrothal twilight zone, the repudiation by the husband would not be a divorce but simply a termination of the contract. In all likelihood, however, the rigor of the ancient laws was no longer strictly adhered to by exception, as indicated by the story of the woman taken in the act of adultery.

Even prior to the angel's advice, Joseph resolved to take a low-key approach and not shame Mary or create a public scandal in the village. As an observer of the law, he felt bound to terminate the engagement, but as a sensitive and compassionate man he sought a private settlement. He would sign the dissolution papers before witnesses but refused to allow any public exposure.

The rescuing angel tells Joseph that God's Spirit is the cause of Mary's pregnancy. The angel even gives orders about naming the boy Jesus, which means savior. Just as the hero-warrior Joshua saved ancient Israel from the dead end of wandering to oblivion in the

Sinai wastes and led her into the promised land, so the new Yeshua/Jesus would lead all men away from sin and into the hope-laden new kingdom of his Father.

The angel reminds Joseph that Jesus will be born of a virgin and that this event is the fulfillment of a prophecy found in Isaiah 7:14. This is the first of eleven prophecy fulfillment texts to be found in Matthew's gospel. Matthew's preoccupation with prophetic predictions, greater than in the other three gospels combined, requires some consideration.

Popular belief long associated prophets with predictions, even though most of their preaching dwelt on the evils of idolatry and injustice and the consequent need for conversion, penance and reform. The social upheavals of the 1960s brought to the fore the image of the prophet as moral reformer and paid little attention to his role as predictor. Some enthusiasts even dismissed the foretelling role as irrelevant sacred fortune-telling in order to fuel a stronger commitment to social reform. It is perhaps inevitable that similar exaggerations will continue to crop up.

Matthew stresses the ability of prophets to forecast the future. Far-seeing persons are present in every age. People ahead of their times often give uncannily accurate predictions concerning the future. This occurs both in science fiction and the discipline of futurology. The stress on prophets' ability to forecast should not, however, obscure their other role as social reformers and stirrers of the human conscience.

Matthew quotes from Isaiah 7:14: "Therefore the Lord himself will give you this sign: the Virgin shall be with child, and bear a son, and shall name him Immanuel." Matthew sees this prophecy fulfilled in two ways: Mary the Virgin giving birth, and Jesus as the Immanuel.

In recent years this text has prompted a discussion about the virginity of Mary. The original Hebrew text of Isaiah used the word *Almah*, meaning "a young girl," not necessarily a virgin. When the Hebrew text was translated into Greek by the Septuagint scholars, they used the word *Parthenos*, meaning "virgin." Matthew followed this Greek translation.

No one is sure why they did this. Some church fathers attributed the change to divine inspiration. Others speculated that the translators were influenced by Greek religious thoughts, which possessed a strand of tradition about virginal conception of savior figures.

The critics, observing this, concluded that it was a mistake for Matthew to use this as a fulfillment text since the original does not refer to a virgin. But neither does the original exclude the possibility of the young girl being virginal, and moreover, this *felix culpa* ("happy accident") of the Greek translation coincided with the faith statement of Matthew.

Aside from these language arguments, more serious doubts about Mary's virginity have surfaced. Skeptics deny it altogether. A new element is a creeping doubt among some Christian believers, a feeling that it is somehow unfitting that a truly incarnated Jesus should not be sired by a human father. Or, as the argument goes: Can he be truly human if he was not the offspring of a human couple?

Since God is the origin of all that is human, its creator, why is it unthinkable that the Spirit could have acted in a mysterious way at the time of Jesus' conception? Surely the virgin birth is no greater obstacle to faith than the resurrection. If Jesus concluded his earthly life with the remarkable miracle of triumphing over death, why couldn't he have entered this life in an equally unique manner? Isn't it perhaps more fitting that he come this way than to have been born of parents in a regular manner? The argument about what is fitting can be cut two ways. Virgin birth, like resurrection, is an object of faith, not of scientific observation.

Today, it is popular to use the word myth to deny what one prefers not to believe. Because much biblical talk is poetic and does not record facts in our sense of the word—the assumption grows that there may be no core of historical happening at all. But the word myth basically refers to a poetic way of saying something. It can mean either a poetic way of relating a historical event or a pretty way of speaking about a fictional happening. The problem of the biblical scholar is to determine whether the mythical/poetic narrative describes a historical event or a parable with a religious message. When dealing with the virgin birth, we are faced with the weight of Christian tradition which clearly sees it as a faith reality and not as fictional detail or a merely symbolic parable.

The gospel writers did not invent details from the life of Jesus to fit Old Testament texts. They used existing prophecies to illuminate what they saw and believed about Jesus. Matthew begins with Jesus and then notes how biblical tradition points toward his coming. He is saying that Jesus is indeed Immanuel, God fully with us.

Reflection

1. What value do I find in exploring the roots of my own family?
2. Matthew connects Jesus to David. Do I derive a special feeling of greatness from one or other of my forebears?
3. Matthew includes some embarrassing ancestors in Christ's family tree. What do I think of the "black sheep" in my ancestry?
4. Angels appear in biblical dreams. Do I sometimes acquire spiritual insight from my dreams?
5. Joseph planned to terminate his engagement to Mary in a low-key and sensitive way. How do I react to broken engagements among relatives and friends?
6. Prophets interpret God's will in society. They also sometimes predict the future. Do I see prophets in today's church and society?
7. Matthew affirms Mary's virginity in begetting Jesus. The church teaches Mary's perpetual virginity. What do I believe to be the value of virginity in today's erotic-oriented society?
8. Do I experience Christ's call to faith in this narrative?
9. Does my faith ask me to make difficult decisions?
10. What does Joseph's example teach me in this story?

Prayer

Loving Father, I thank you for the gift of the Incarnation. I praise you for the sensitivity and faith of St. Joseph toward Blessed Mary. I pray for an understanding and forgiving nature whenever I face someone who appears to be a problem to me. I believe, dear Father. Help my unbelief.

2 Wise Men at Worship

Star of Wonder (Mt. 2:1-8)

Jesus was born in Bethlehem, a small town six miles south of Jerusalem. Bethlehem means House of Bread. The town may have been small but its walls had witnessed much history. Jacob buried his wife Rachel there. Its most famous son, prior to Jesus, was David. Thus, this quiet hamlet has been the scene of two royal births, those of David and Jesus.

Tradition has identified a hillside cave as the birthplace of Christ. In the fourth century, Constantine built the church of the Nativity over and around the cave to preserve it as a shrine. It is situated beneath the main altar and numerous silver lamps reflect the gold star on the floor of the small chamber. A simple inscription surrounds the star: "Here was Jesus Christ born of the Virgin Mary."

Luke tells the story of poor Jewish shepherds coming to worship Christ. Matthew, however, recalls the adoration of the Magi, gentile wise men from the east. The Magi belonged to a priestly caste in Persia where their principal task was to be intellectual and religious advisers to the Persian kings. They were trained in philosophy, medicine and, above all, in the study of the stars.

Our present space age has recaptured a fascination with the stars and planets and even with the reading of horoscopes. The stars also captivated the ancients. The common belief was that at birth each person was represented by a star. To be born under a lucky star is still a popular saying. Each night, the regular pattern of these celestial lights presented to the upturned eye, the reassurance of order and purpose in the universe.

Obviously, any change in the night sky raised questions on earth, especially for such trained observers as the Magi. Comets, shooting stars, eclipses, confluences of planets or the appearance of a new star, automatically prompted wonder and lengthy discussion. Matthew states that just such an astral spectacular set the Persian Magi community to pondering its significance.

They came to what was considered the normal conclusion, that it signified the birth of an exceptional person. They were well aware of the spirit of the times which anticipated the appearance of some remarkable savior figure. The caravans that came to Persia from the west brought more than goods to be traded. They communicated the news of the Roman Empire and the stories of contemporary yearning. The Magi would have known of the poet Virgil's fourth eclogue which prophesied the coming of a golden age. They would have been struck by the fact that the new emperor, Augustus, was being hailed as the savior of the world. But, clearly, what impressed them more than anything was the persistent refrain coming from Palestine that a messiah most certainly was soon to appear.

The Jewish monks at the monastery of Qumran along the shores of the Dead Sea preached that a Teacher of Righteousness would most likely emerge at any time to usher in the promised Last Days and the arrival of the kingdom of God. This news, coupled with all the rest, persuaded some of the Persian wise men that the starry epiphany referred to the Jewish Messiah.

Laden with gifts, they set out for Jerusalem to find this child of wonder. Legend has supplied details not included in Matthew's text. Tradition pictures the Magi as kings and names them Caspar, Melchior and Balthasar. Christmas cards, faithful to that tradition, portray Melchior as the grandfather type, offering the gold. Next to him stands the youthful Caspar, presenting the frankincense. Last comes the dark-skinned Balthasar with his gift of myrrh.

Some critics have dismissed the story of the Magi as a myth, a lovely poetic tale with no basis in fact. They argue that it appears nowhere else in ancient literature and that it is simply a beautiful story used by Matthew to relate that Christ was born to save gentiles as well as Jews.

Yet, the event is precisely the kind of thing that could have happened. The beauty of the Magi is that they sensed it would not be Augustus who would usher in the golden age predicted by Virgil. For that nothing less than a God was needed. The Magi's meditations on the stars brought them to the presence of the divine. Their natural science and open hearts and minds revealed to them what the custodians of the ancient covenant and scriptures failed to see. Correctly and innocently, they go to Herod, the Roman appointed ruler of Palestine. They confide their news to a king noted for immense contradictions. He had been able to maintain law and order in Palestine where all others had failed. He had built the Temple in Jerusalem, canceled taxes in hard times, and used his own finances to feed the starving during the great famine.

He maintained his power, however, at a terrible price. No one could cross him and expect to live. His assassination list probably would have matched well with that of any of the ruthless murderers who have scarred the governments of twentieth-century life. He killed his wife, his mother-in-law, and three of his sons because he suspected they were after his power. Knowing there would be no tears shed at his funeral, he left orders for mass murders to take place on the day of his death so that mourning would accompany his passing.

It was to such a madman that the Magi revealed their news. At this news King Herod became greatly disturbed, and with him all Jerusalem (Mt. 2:3). Herod's terror arose from his insane fear of rivals. All Jerusalem worries with sympathy about the fate of the child. Herod summons the religious scholars who cite Micah 5:2 about Bethlehem being the site of a messianic birth.

The Adoration of the Magi (Mt. 2:9-12)

In some mysterious way, the Magi find Christ among all the newborn infants of Bethlehem. Matthew states that a star guided them. Poetically, he suggests that it moved before them, as the pillar of fire led the Israelites until it rested over the home of Jesus. However it happened, they found Jesus and bowed down before him in worship.

Preachers and saints have found numerous meanings in the gifts. Generally, they see the gold as being offered to Jesus as the Lord who will establish a spiritual kingdom to fulfill humanity's highest potential. His kingdom will not be of this world, dependent on wealth, prestige or political power. Rather, it will be a kingdom of the spirit, calling people to freedom from all forms of materialism, a freedom to appreciate the depths of truth, goodness, beauty, and love.

The gift of frankincense adverts to Christ's priestly role, to his building over the troubled waters and chaos of a divided world and offering everyone the possibility of peace through union with God. Incense has always been a favorite part of religious ritual not only for its practical value of sweetening the air but also because the rising plumes of smoke seem to be visible prayers bridging heaven and earth.

Since Jesus will be like all other human beings in everything but sin, the gift of myrrh announces his future death. It is a somber detail in an otherwise magnificent scene, as though the shadows of Ash Wednesday and Good Friday had already begun to intrude themselves into the joys of the Incarnation.

Church fathers were fond of pointing out that Jesus is first revealed to poor and humble Jewish shepherds and only later to the prosperous intellectuals from Persia. One writer has noted that Jesus disclosed himself to the humble who knew little and to the learned who appreciated that they did not know everything. But the one group who remained blind to his coming were the religious elite of Israel whose very custody of the prophecies should have alerted them to this possibility.

Finding Jesus today requires the simplicity of the shepherds and the wondering, inquiring minds of the Magi. Possession of the scriptures and religious tradition is not enough if these two forces are not permitted to work their grace on the human soul, liberating people from the excesses of complexity and a blind intellectualism that imagines everything is subject to human reason and analysis.

Dreams (Mt. 2:13-15)

Dreams are prominent in these first two chapters of Matthew. Joseph learns through a dream how Mary became pregnant by the Spirit. A dream alerts the Magi to return to Persia by a different route. An angel in a dream advises Joseph to take Mary and Jesus to Egypt and returns in yet another dream to give the signal for going home. Ancient people found it quite easy to accept divine messages in dreams. Today's growth of dream analysis, prompted by Jung and other psychoanalysts, gives us a new respect for the mysterious world of dreams.

The Holy Innocents (Mt. 2:16-18)

Given the deranged mind of Herod, it was inevitable that he would try to kill Jesus. Since he could not tell which baby was the Christ, he ordered all the male babies of Bethlehem to be killed. Assessing the probable size of a village in those days, it is likely that about thirty children were slaughtered.

As usual, Matthew summons an Old Testament text to comment. He hears in the wailing mothers of Bethlehem an echo of Rachel's tears as recalled by Jeremiah 31:15-34. There, the prophet describes the processions of Jewish slave gangs brutally driven by the Babylonians from their Palestinian homeland into exile. Jeremiah portrays Rachel weeping in her grave over this terrible event as they pass by her tomb.

He turns, however, to her grave and offers words of comfort and hope:

Cease your cries of mourning,
Wipe the tears from your eyes.
The sorrow you have shown shall have its reward
They shall return from the enemy's land.

—Jer. 31:16

Matthew's original readers would have known this story and would have understood that beyond the tragedy lay new hope and new life.

Egypt (Mt. 2:19-23)

For years, teachers have delighted both young and old with legends about the life of Christ. One of the best known concerns the flight into Egypt. The Holy Family meets some robbers on the way. Among them is a man named Dismas who is strangely moved by the child and forbids anyone to molest the family. Fearing that he might again be in need of mercy, Dismas asked Jesus to remember him from this day. On Calvary, Jesus would remember him.

The family stayed in Egypt until Herod died, then returned to Nazareth where Jesus grew up watching the world's caravans go by on the great highway near the sea below the hills of his village.

Reflection

1. Do I think I have a lucky star?
2. Why do people read horoscopes?
3. Christ's birthplace is remembered with reverence. Do I have a warm spot in my heart for my birthplace?
4. How would I react if I saw a shooting star, or a sudden change in the night sky?
5. Whom do I consider to be wise persons today? In my family? Among my friends? In society?
6. What impresses me most about the Magi?
7. Gold, frankincense and myrrh have spiritual meanings. What three personal gifts would I offer Jesus today?
8. Jesus revealed himself to humble shepherds and prestigious wise men. Both were open enough to recognize him as the Savior. Do I have the openness to recognize Jesus in my life?
9. Some believe the Feast of the Holy Innocents would be a good time to have a Day of Prayer to stop abortions. What do I think?
10. What can I do to protect innocent children from being mistreated or abused?

Prayer

Jesus, your life was threatened very soon after you were born. Your parents protected you by becoming refugees in Egypt. I see many pictures of neglected and abandoned children. I ask for the strength and wisdom to do whatever I can to eliminate abortion and help children in need. Fill me with the love that makes this possible.

3   How to Be Evangelical

The Call to Conversion (Mt. 3:1-12)

It is never easy to have a good conscience, and people left to themselves find it even more difficult. Fortunately, God never leaves them alone long enough to lapse into indifference. All recorded religious history rings with the cry of conscience stingers. The Old Testament called them prophets. The New Testament described them as evangelical apostles. Church history tends to call them saints. America developed the protestant revival preacher and the Catholic missioner who in pre-Vatican Council days took a strong line on sin and repentance. The 1960s witnessed the social reformer as yet another variation of the conscience improver.

John the Baptist ranks as one of the greatest of consciousness raisers. Dressed like Elijah of old in a sandpapery camel hide and living on a diet so restricted that even today's macrobiotic advocates would feel hungry, he assailed the complacent of his age. Preachers normally have a double role: to comfort the afflicted and to afflict the comfortable. Without doubt, John chose the latter. Four centuries had passed since Palestine had sensed it had anything approaching a genuine prophet of the stature of Isaiah or Amos. Few contested that John the Baptist more than deserved the title of prophet of the Lord. He wasted no time on crowd pleasing techniques. Perhaps he scored low in tact, but he achieved the highest grades in candor and honesty. He suffered no credibility gap.

Never one to hide his intentions, he declared himself on a number of issues. He told the soldiers of occupation that they should be ashamed of themselves for brutalizing the weak. He accused the tax authorities of cheating, graft and other unfair collection practices. He remonstrated with the religious leaders for being mere functionaries who hid behind their official status and thwarted the possibilities of real religion.

John did not spare the rank and file believers either. He knew that they had become stale in their religion, that they were relying on an inherited faith and were secretly arrogant about being children of Abraham. Like a seedy aristocrat who boasts about lineage, many of his listeners were faded heirs of the glorious faith of Abraham. The fire had gone out in their hearts. Matthew shows only John's attack on the religious leaders. One also should read Luke's version of the Baptist's sermons (Luke 3:7-38).

Religious believers of every age need the shake-up that only a Baptist can provide. Much of religious lethargy comes from forgetting the whole point of faith and the life that goes with it. Self-indulgence and the rationalizing of all behavior breeds the loss of a sense of faith and soon enables one to explain away all possibility of sin.

If there is no faith and belief in God there will soon be no need to be responsible for one's personal behavior. Reason and common sense call for responsibility but, somehow, unless the religious motivation is present together with the awareness that the power of God is needed to remain conscientious and responsible, there usually is a mass indifference to morality.

If John the Baptist were alive today he would most likely make a sharp attack on those who would attempt to reduce human accountability by misusing the findings of psychology and sociology as an excuse or rationalization for their inappropriate actions. The Baptist would agree that psychological pressures and environmental obstacles take their toll in terms of the quality of human behavior, but he would never concur that this should always eliminate responsibility for one's actions.

John refused to let the official roles of the military or the church obscure the moral responsibility of the people of his time. He would not allow the members of his congregation to employ religious and cultural bloodlines to escape the call of God to live noble and fulfilling lives. Today, he probably would be a famous person, though not altogether well-liked. His words would strike too close to home for many people. He would speak of sin and God's moral order and the need to repent.

Repentance is a central feature of the Baptist's program. The word comes from a Greek term meaning a change of one's life, a personal reform. As an evangelical preacher, John did not flinch in making a radical demand upon his listeners. He would not tolerate the doctrine of doing one's own thing, which is often only an excuse for self-indulgence. For those who can remember such things, he would probably come across as a fire and brimstone speaker.

He would be facing congregations that have known the impact of the Death of God Movement, declines in church attendance, situation ethics, foreign missionaries who are embarrassed to speak of Christ, and a vague romantic love morality that reduces love to one of its sentimental components. In the midst of this, his voice would come loud and clear—probably disagreeable as well: Repent! Change! Take responsibility for your acts. Recover a sense of norms and laws in the moral order. Do not let every moral and religious belief die the death of a thousand qualifications.

John could be nasty. He called his congregation a brood of snakes running from the avenging fire. He was a shaker and a mover and there is no reason to doubt that he would be equally pointed today. What enabled him to avoid self-righteousness was that he both lived what he believed and had a strong positive side to his message.

His personal lifestyle, clearly ascetic, set him apart from any self-serving ambition. He could be as impudent to King Herod as to any local citizen for he had no designs on power and little regard for popularity polls. He was a free man. He was not Elmer Gantry preaching self-denial while practicing self indulgence. He had nothing to lose because there was not a grasping cell within him. He proclaimed a bold, positive message: Be baptized for the kingdom of God is at hand. He was saying that the gift of grace stood ahead for those who would turn from the old ways and open their hearts to the Lord. They could be born again, as Christ later was to say. The baptismal washing served as a public pledge that the person was willing to walk in a new life. Interior change deserved a visible ceremony.

Water is a destructive, cleansing and regenerating agent. The flood waters in the time of Noah destroyed the sinners of the earth. The cleansing river purified the leprosy of Naaman in the time of Elijah. Water everywhere quenches thirst, gives life to human hearts. John called upon the people to immerse themselves in Jordan's waters and to destroy their old ways, cleanse their hearts and prepare themselves for the new creation in Christ.

The Baptism of Jesus (Mt. 3:13-17)

The whole point of the Baptist's message was that we should move away from sin and turn to the grace that comes in Christ. Now, Jesus himself comes to participate in the baptismal ceremony. He shows the need for purification. If he, the innocent, the sinless one, can publicly go through the ceremony of moral cleansing, then why should those who really need it not do so?

Jesus accepts the baptism of John not only in order to encourage the Baptist's mission of repentance and baptism, but also to signal the beginning of his own evangelical career. All four gospels note that the start of his public ministry takes place at the Jordan. The baptism by water is accompanied by a divine anointing of the Spirit and the liturgical words of the Father confirming the sonship of Jesus.

They are from Psalm 2. The imagery of the Spirit over the water and God's Son comes from a tapestry of poems written by Isaiah about the Old Testament servant of God who would bring peace and justice to the nations:

Here is my servant whom I uphold
My chosen one with whom I am pleased,
Upon whom I have put my Spirit;
He shall bring forth justice to the nations.

—Is. 42:1-2

Thus we see Jesus as God-Son and Servant, one who will bring to fulfillment the hopes of all the prophets and especially the new dreams stirred up by John the Baptist, the final heir of Hebrew prophecy. Jesus, too, in the evangelical spirit of John, will make repentance a core of the message. He will insist that the kingdom of Heaven is at hand. God's rule will be more clearly manifest to the whole world and no one will be immune to the possibility that the kingdom offers.

The assumption is that the world has too long been under the rule of evil. The powers of darkness have had their way for too long. It is time to overthrow evil once and for all. One of the main purposes of Christ's ministry will be to demonstrate to his listeners that evil does not have to triumph, that it can be vanquished, that hope, and integrity, and peace, and love are values that are achievable and that

God's reign will make them enduring and lasting possibilities for everyone.

Reflection

1. Some people are uneasy about legends. Yet did I not benefit from fairy tales as a child? As an adult, could I not learn something from short stories and novels that have a wholesome message?
2. Is there anyone I know that arouses my conscience?
3. Have I come across a "John the Baptizer Type" in my milieu?
4. If I meet a conscience arouser who has no tact but lots of integrity, will I listen to such a messenger?
5. Do I think regular church attenders need to be shaken up once in a while? On what issues?
6. What is the biggest reason for religious lethargy?
7. John called for repentance. Have I felt the need to repent of something in my life? Do I need moral conversion?
8. What can I learn from the baptism of Jesus?
9. Why do I need the Sacrament of Reconciliation as part of my conversion/repentance process?
10. Have I lost my recognition of sin in my life? How can I regain it and then go onto repentance and conversion?

Prayer

Have mercy on me, God, in your compassion. I see my sins before me and the evil I have done. If you purify me, I shall be made clean. If you wash me, I shall be whiter than snow. Fill me again with the joy of your forgiving and helping presence. Teach me a state of the heart morality, so that my heart will always be pure. You can blot out my guilt. I open my heart to receive your cleansing grace.

4 The Devil Did Not Make Him Do It

Removing evil from the world is no easy matter. At the time of the Garden of Eden there might have been two ways to prevent evil from occurring, namely, to get rid of the serpent so that no temptation would assail Adam or, to change Adam's heart so that it would not matter what the serpent did. Such either/or solutions do not work. In the real world there are serpents and weak characters.

The continuous battle is to drive out the serpents and to cleanse human hearts.

The story of Christ's testing in the Judean wilderness is a case study of a real world where the seductive forces of evil from without try to wither the integrity of the human heart within. Jesus faces up to the battle and portrays for us the model behavior that makes temptation a fruitful occasion for growth. It is not a matter of a reckless confrontation but of refusing to live a hot-house existence in which inner strength can never be developed. The careers of outstanding leaders almost always reveal that withdrawal and contemplation are part of development. The Spirit moves Jesus away from the crowds to the silences of the desert. A leader is a person who undergoes the experiences of his people in a unique and thorough way. Those experiences need to be absorbed and reflected upon in solitude.

Jesus shows the way by spending time in retreat. This call of the Spirit remains a valid gospel demand to this day. Self-imposed silence, meditation and examination of one's life is a classic road to spiritual renewal just as the current fad for public self-analysis is a dead end.

The cleansing of the heart begun by repentance and baptism needs the renewal offered by retreat. Evil is not overcome easily.

Speaking of this age, William Butler Yeats wrote: "The center cannot hold. The best lack all conviction. The worst are full of passionate intensity."[*] The best should not lack conviction. If they do, it is an era that pretends evil is nonexistent and opts for a so-called wholesome degeneracy.

The moral level of a culture depends upon the spiritual quality of its citizens. Without the perspective provided by occasional withdrawal from the noise-pollution of modern life, can anyone really expect to possess the spiritual strength required for creating a just and humane society? Jesus went to the desert both to get away from the noise of the Jordan and to face the tests that all spiritual maturing demands.

Three Temptations (Mt. 4:1-11)

What follows is an imaginary reconstruction of the temptation stories, in the form of a play.

Act I

Satan: I see you are hungry. You are foolish to put such stock in fasting. You shouldn't believe those who tell you it is good for the soul. Actually, it does little good for your personality. It just ruins your disposition. I'm told that you are God's Love Child. Why not satisfy yourself? After all, you have the means. Turn these stones that look like loaves into bread.

Jesus: The beauty of fasting is that it sharpens my insight. I can see you for what you are, a father of lies. If my disposition becomes querulous, it's not because I'm hungry. It's due to my anger at your deceptiveness. Bread alone isn't everything. You support material satisfaction to mask spiritual starvation. Man also lives by the strength that comes from God's word.

Satan: I don't believe you. I think you hunger for happiness and self-satisfaction just like anyone else. You ought to take the shortcut since you so easily can. Use an anesthetic. Get instant relief. Do nothing slowly.

[*] William B. Yeats, "The Second Coming," *The Norton Anthology of Poetry* (New York: W. W. Norton Co., 1970), p. 915.

Jesus: The bread of instant satisfaction will not insure true self-development. It distracts from the origin of genuine self-realization and maturing. The inability to defer gratification is childishness. I teach that great demands make great people. The eternal word of God comes but slowly and with effort to live regularly in human consciousness.

Act II

Satan: Walk with me to the temple. . . Now, join me in the climb to the high tower. See behind us the 450-foot drop into the Kedron valley. You know this is where the temple priest stands each morning and blows on the *shofar* (ram's horn) when the first glint of dawn hits the Hebron hills. He calls the people to sacrifices.

Jesus: I don't need any instruction about temple liturgies. You are not talking to a tourist. What's on your mind now?

Satan: It's evident to me that you are a born religious leader. But you need to do something dramatic to gain people's attention. Look at the crowds down there in the temple court. Jump from this tower. Descend from the heavens. Didn't the prophet Daniel say you would come in the clouds of heaven? Don't worry, the angels will cushion your fall.

Jesus: It is evil to force God's hand. I won't tempt him and neither should you. It is in the ordinary that the extraordinary will be found. You cheapen the very scriptures you quote.

Satan: Nevertheless, I know that all religious leaders are fond of gimmicks. You can't expect to reach people without something catchy. Your method is your message after all. You must learn how to woo people. As I said, don't worry. Angels will cushion your fall.

Jesus: It is wrong to think that my primary work is to amuse people with tricks. The true way to the divine is honest and sincere leveling with people. You cannot tempt people or God with programs. I know the value of method and program but I see them as part of a goal. Don't forget that a good thing begins small and grows slowly. You want me to build idols in the temple. I call my people to the living God.

Act III

Satan: Hike with me to the summit of the Mount of Olives. There, look at the splendor of Jerusalem, the gold of the temple the spacious courts of Herod's imperial palace.

Jesus: I have seen this many times. What is on your mind now?

Satan: Beyond the seas are kingdoms and cities far more marvelous than this! Alexandria, Athens, Carthage, and Rome. You want a better life for the people who will follow you. The only way to achieve that is to get power. I see your incredible talent. I can teach you how to use it to take over the very throne of Caesar. Stick with me and I will give you an everlasting name.

Jesus: I do not seek such power. It corrupts those who reach for it. And absolute power corrupts absolutely. You offer a power where the strong bewilder the weak. If there must be power, let it be the moral and spiritual power that comes from God. I will not bruise the tender reed.

Satan: You're wrong. You're denying your own possibilities. If you don't listen to me, you will fail and your beloved poor will get nothing. Put yourself in my hands. Commit yourself to me with the very strength of adoration. I hold greatness before you. I can offer it to you now.

Jesus: Never! You lie. You don't know me and you don't know my people. You would destroy us both. In your own perverse way you have taught me a lesson: I shall disdain the cheap dramatic gesture. I shall never claw for power. That is the grand illusion that would corrupt my quest. Begone! Get out! God. God. Abba. Father . . . help me.

And angels came and comforted him.

In the furnace of the desert solitude Jesus completed the preparation for his mission. Following that preparation, he strides forth into Galilee to begin the messianic times. He does not point to himself as the messiah but rather proclaims the arrival of the kingdom of Heaven. He does not refer to a kingdom of God because he shares with his Jewish culture the reverence for the divine name which should rarely be uttered lest it be cheapened.

The rule of God is already present in Jesus. The remainder of his career will be devoted to working for its visible appearance and practical results in people's lives. While the kingdom is spiritual and, therefore, invisible, it must assume a public shape in a visible community. The external form is not to be political or territorial. It is the bringing to fullness of human potential. After all, when God said, "Let there be Man" (Gn. 1:26), God was perfectly aware of what that command meant and what people could become.

It is not God's will that people remain frustrated and undeveloped. The kingdom of Heaven that Jesus preaches involves what humanity can become in the widest sense of maturity and spiritual transcendence. To those who today would say that one does not need Christ's Kingdom to become fully human, the Lord's reply is that there is no other way. Only the Maker knows the full potential of humanity — refusal to listen and accept is to remain forever unmade and incomplete.

Reflection

1. Should I blame my upbringing and pressures from today's society for my sins?
2. The song, "Put the Blame on Me," is entertaining. Why is it poor moral advice?
3. What moves me most about the fact that Jesus allowed himself to be tempted to sin?
4. Jesus made a retreat in the desert. How often do I make a retreat or take time away from my busy life to examine myself?
5. I may have tried dieting. Have I tried fasting for my spiritual growth? Am I as good at nourishing my soul as my body?
6. In my prayers, do I try to force God's hand? Do I want everything my way, even in prayer? How do I understand God's will?
7. Am I a power seeker? Do I have high control needs in my family? With my friends? In the workplace?
8. How do I handle the temptations in my life? Do I have a support group? What role does my faith play?
9. Jesus went to the furnace of solitude to prepare for his mission. What is my attitude about solitude? *alone but not lonely*
10. Jesus was the living kingdom of God. How can I let that kingdom grow within me?

Prayer

Jesus, I often think of how sinful and bad other people are. I dwell on their imperfections, faults and how easily they give into temptation. "Why can't they change?" I think to myself. Turn my attention to my own heart and its laxness in dealing with temptation. Motivate me to take the log from my own eye before removing the splinter from someone else's. Defend me from the tempter.

5 The Sermon on the Mount

One of the attractive features of Matthew's gospel is its neat structure, with five blocks of Christ's sermons interspersed with five sections of stories. The first block of sayings, known as the Sermon on the Mount, is perhaps the most attractive collection of all sayings of Jesus. The material in chapters five to seven is a gathering of his core sayings and homilies. Matthew pictures him as delivering this "New Torah/Law" on a mountain in order to identify Jesus with Moses, the great lawgiver of Israel.

The numerous prescriptions of these three chapters ought not to be read in a legalistic spirit as though they could be obeyed by anyone as easily as he submits to traffic ordinances or other laws of the state. Jesus is announcing the absolute ideals of the kingdom of God. He gives us standards whereby to measure conduct, and offers a series of radical demands that stretch the human soul to its fullest potential. He speaks of the quality of action and the goals to which spiritual life must aspire.

Achieving the ideals of this sermon will take the grace assisted human a lifetime. In modern psychological terms, it provides the framework for the development of the human person through progressive stages of maturity. It illustrates what the poet Robert Browning meant when he wrote of the need for heaven to be beyond man's reach: "Else what's a heaven for?"[*]

The sermon is immensely rich and it is impossible to give an exhaustive and complete commentary here. The following discussion attempts simply to extract ten imperatives that seem to characterize sections of the sermon and to give direction for further meditation. In his sonnets William Shakespeare writes of his beloved: "Shall I com-

[*] Robert Browning, "Andrea Del Sarto," *The Norton Anthology of Poetry* (New York: W. W. Norton Co., 1970) p. 780.

pare thee to a summer's day?" He answers his own question: "No, you are more wonderful by far." So it is with this incomparable sermon, richer than any words about it.

Be a Kingdom Person (Mt. 5:1-12)

In the Beatitudes, which begin the sermon, Jesus offers eight qualities that will mark those who know what it is like to be a kingdom person. Because he is speaking of a spiritual kingdom, he outlines characteristics and values that often reverse the hallmarks of the successful worldly person. He includes no practices of piety in the list. This is not because he has no regard for religious practices. Rather, it is because he is making a central distinction between means and ends. The eight values are ends and goals. Practices of piety are means to such goals.

Poor in Spirit. This value does not refer to checking accounts or possessions. It is about radical dependence upon God, the knowledge that all we own, we owe. It is very much related to the first commandment of Sinai: Trust in no false gods. Throw over any idols from which no help can come. Human pride in personal achievement gradually erodes the memory that nothing is ultimately possible without God's continuing power and presence. Only kingdom people know this secret. They are aware of their achievements and the results of their efforts. But, because they always see the ultimate aspect of what they do, they are freed from jealousy and possessiveness and are therefore capable of inheriting the whole earth.

The Meek. This value has nothing to do with timidity. Perhaps hard-core gentleness is more to the point. It is related to humility, which derives from the Latin word for earth. This is the value of the earthy person, the thorough realist, conscious of dependence upon God, aware of God's abiding kindness. Humble, hard core gentleness is not romantic passivity, but a bold tact and abiding sympathy for the human condition. These gentle persons have plenty of courage and daring, but they never lose the warmth that comes from proximity to the Fire.

The Mourners. Life on earth will always be a mixture of triumph and tragedy, laughter and tears. Pain and disappointment are always with us. For kingdom people, the point is that they never lose a sensitivity to evil and its impact, whether at a personal or universal level. They deny the old saying that if you cry, you cry all alone. They will let no one cry alone, for they will be there to lend empathy and hope.

Hunger for Holiness. Every human heart possesses the unrestricted drive to be at one with the infinite God. Augustine called it "the restless heart" that would not be calm until it rests in God. Francis Thompson's poem about God as the "Hound of Heaven" who chases us until we give in to God's loving advance is another aspect. The real kingdom person discovers this inner hunger planted there by God and begins to realize the excitement of a drive that is deeper than the thrust to food, and sex, and power. If psychiatrist Adler speaks of Friedrick Nietzsche's "Will to Power," the Beatitude-value dwells on the Will to God.

The Merciful. God is the supreme Master of forgiveness. Mercy means giving before the possibility of acceptance. It is not a question of waiting for apologies and then being magnanimous. The fore-giver is *already* offering acceptance before repentance takes place. It is precisely because of this prior attitude of mercy that apology and repentance is even thinkable. Fore-giveness is the condition for the possibility of reconciliation. Kingdom persons know this instinctively and are the divine gift to all who secretly wish to reform their lives.

Peacemakers. In a world where violence, wars, quarrels, murders and fights are daily occurrences, there is a special need for this kind of kingdom person. A peacemaker is a gift to a family, to a community, and to a nation. Only one in whom the grace of Christ burns with special fervor can hope to realize the extent of energy, imagination, and flexibility required to be a peacemaker.

The Pure in Heart. The old moralistic history books were fond of telling the story of Sir Galahad, who had the strength of ten because his heart was pure. It subsequently became the fashion to dismiss this as a foolish tale. It was better to get down to the real facts of the case. But this is a worldly view. Kingdom people are mighty because of their integrity of heart and purity of intention. One may argue that no motivations are ever that pure. That is possible, but the ideal is being invoked and the dream is drawing kingdom persons to achieve it with God's grace.

The Persecuted. All great people will suffer for their principles in one way or another. It is the substance of which martyrdom is made. There are times when compromise is impossible and a stand must be taken. This is not a question of futile rushing in where angels fear to tread. It is exactly where angels boldly march. It is the meaning of the Cross of Jesus and the dungeon, fire and sword that become the lot of all kingdom persons who stand up for their faith.

These values are guiding stars. Sailors cannot reach up and put stars in their pockets. But the star can lead them to their destination. These values offer the means by which kingdom persons can develop into their full capability.

Honor Tradition (Mt. 5:13-20)

Without roots there is no tree. But without the tree the roots remain dead anachronisms. In revolutionary times there is often a disdain for tradition. The new kingdom announced by Jesus has a revolutionary ring to it, but Jesus does not want to abolish the law and the prophets: He came not to abolish them, but to fulfill them (5:17). For the remainder of chapter five, Matthew recalls how Jesus took a tradition and infused into it a new life and meaning: when he reports that Christ said not only have we heard it rumored . . . but he tells us (6:21-22).

The devil that plagues many reformers in religion is that they forget history. The democracy of the dead means nothing to them. That is one of the reasons why a certain fanaticism seems to take hold of some. They will create the perfect church for the first time in history. Reformers in the sixteenth century rightfully wanted to purify the church. Their criticisms of church abuses, including their accusations about ecclesiastical cruelty, were legitimate. Yet, some of them went on to repeat similar horrors, among them the slaughter of such other reformers as the Anabaptists.

They preached freedom, but were occasionally the first to exile any dissenters. They forgot a traditional saying of the Italians: Where the weeds grow, the wheat grows too. The impulse to perfectionism appeared among some reformers in the 1960s in the midst of some very wholesome reforms and renewals. This was especially evident in talk about holy remnants, a phrase adopted from the Old Testament prophets who predicted that most of Israel would be lost and dispersed in scattered exile but that a holy remnant would survive to preserve the ancient faith and bring it home again one day.

The thought is salutary. The problem of its use in the present situation is the self-congratulatory use made of it by a self-proclaimed elite who would save the church while all else went their blind ways. It is quite possible that a small remnant eventually will be the result of all the renewal. The question here is not to pontificate on its possibility but to call in question those who claim to be charter members in advance. The sense of tradition of those who would save us all is often numb. They have forgotten the past and reserved a space for first class in the presumably enlightened future.

Jesus is bringing tradition to fulfillment. He proclaims ideals but is aware that the community of faith will have sinners and weak ones until the end of time. He had only to look at his own apostles, with their abiding, and sometimes engaging, foibles to realize that the regular citizens of the family of believers will be a tenuous group of persons.

Jesus' fulfilling ideals are spiritual depths implied by the ancient Torah. It spoke against murder. Jesus deepened it to mean that any unresolved hostile anger is a sin against Torah. It denounced adultery. Jesus insisted that a lustful heart is equally deserving of condemnation. It railed against false oaths. Jesus reminded them that using legitimate oaths to avoid moral responsibilities was equally hateful.

Respect Persons (Mt. 5:21-42)

The major philosophy of the late twentieth century is personalism. It calls for seeing the uniqueness of persons and therefore avoiding stereotypes or translating everyone into some form of abstract ideas. Martin Buber stressed the need for an I-Thou relationship in which we would not use others as things, but treat them as persons, centers of meaning and love, deserving of respect. Personalism espouses the idea that people are the greatest of all masterpieces. Cultivated people revere a work of art but often ignore or revile the artist. Let Mozart starve, but enjoy his symphonies. Exclaim rapturously over Picasso's Guernica but expend little if any compassion for the brutalized people the painting depicts. Push urban renewal so the middle class will have nice neighborhoods to drive through on their way to work, but ignore the poor and the deprived who are pushed out of the way for the freeways and fancy shops.

To paraphrase Joseph Stalin, one death is a tragedy; a million deaths are a statistic. Personalism insists that all deaths are part of the human tragedy and that the pity is that even one death now seems to have lost its power to shock.

Jesus speaks of the need to discover one's brother and sister as persons. It is necessary to overcome the anger that wipes out the other, and imperative not to stereotype them by calling them "Raca" (Mt. 5:22). Modern forms of "Raca" occur in racial, ethnic and sexist slurs — too painful to explicitly mention here — that often wound people deeply. Somehow, the use of the put-down label reduces the other to a thing and ignores the divine masterpiece, the person, of whom Jesus speaks.

It is important to note that Raca behavior appears at all levels of education and sophistication. It is not the special province of street talk. It appears in chic condominiums and Ivy league doctoral seminars and plush board rooms. It is practiced both by people wearing open neck denim shirts and those in white on white linen and grey herringbone suits.

No one is exempt from the sin of depersonalization. It often seems as though all people can be happy only if they have someone to look down on. Such people would never understand what it means to learn something from every person they meet, and they certainly must be puzzled to know that Will Rogers said that he never met a person he didn't like.

Jesus goes on to say that people should leave their gifts at the altar until they have made up with another with whom they are at odds. Secular critics of religion love to harp on the Sunday churchgoer who is a liar and a cheat for the rest of the week. It is a criticism that remains regularly and legitimately valid — though one can only hope that the critics themselves are immune from the hypocrisy they condemn.

In the ideal order, real worship should be an act of adoration by a community of believers. It is not going to be a community unless each member of the congregation is aware of the need to respect everyone as a person. Titles, offices and status must not get in the way of seeing the person. This was the whole idea behind asking Christians to see the Christ in each other. Jesus is the perfection of one's personhood in the sense that union with him means reaching for the fullness of personal maturity. Being in love with Christ assures the full flowering of personhood.

But labels do get in the way. People need status and label as a crutch. There is nothing wrong with a crutch to start things off. But the day must come when one can walk freely as a person, throw away the crutch and leap and dance like a cured lame person.

I'm nobody, who are you?
Are you nobody, too?
Sh, don't tell anyone, they'll banish us, you know.
How dreadful to be somebody,
Barking your name all day to an admiring bog.

—Emily Dickinson

She is contrasting the nobodies with the somebodies of the world. By "nobody" she means a man or woman who has discovered that unique personhood is the greatest of all gifts. Titles such as general, president or professor or status such as executive, film star, or chairman of the board have a certain value. They indicate that you are a "somebody." But if you are not a real person, then what good is the title or the status? Emily Dickinson is not against the somebodies per se, but she is insisting that in the last analysis personhood is more important.

This is the point of Christ's personalized statements in the Sermon on the Mount. He asks us to test our Raca quotient — to test how much we humiliate others with epithets and demeaning stereotypes. He wants real persons at worship, not those who hold grudges and thus reduce neighbors to things.

Love Your Enemies (Mt. 5:43-48)

The *Imitation of Christ* suggests that we should look closely at our enemies, for in them we first discover our faults. Shakespeare suggests that enemies are our outward consciences. All people of common sense learn a great deal from their enemies, often far more than they do from their friends. There is more than humor in Oscar Wilde's comment: "A man cannot be too careful in the choice of his enemies."[*] This is probably the wisdom behind the proverb that says you can save yourself from your enemies, but it would take God to defend you from your friends.

Jesus asks us to love our enemies. Doubtless he had in mind the pervasive wisdom implied in the above statements. He may also be thinking in terms of the sign that hangs in many offices: "Love your enemies. It will drive them crazy."

Jesus wants us to love our enemies, however, not just because they are walking psycho charts reminding us of our own ridiculousness, but also in order that we will create the possibilities of reconciliation. He speaks here of the highest form of love. Other forms, such as self love and contract love, are certainly important too. Self love abolishes self hatred and the paralysis that comes from it. (I am not referring here to the self love that can be selfishness.)

Contract love deals with the bartering of good deeds in a manner reminiscent of the exchange of Christmas gifts. Creative love, the highest form, produces love where it has not existed before. Jesus is saying we cannot afford the luxury of an enemy because of the well known consequences of hostility, quarrels, fights, wars, beatings, tortures, and all other forms of dehumanization.

Spiritual writers call this love a theological virtue because it is a love so great that only God can assist us with it. As the supreme value that we must learn to make our own, this creative love will be the dominant quality of a kingdom person.

[*] John P. Bradley, comp., *International Dictionary of Thoughts* (Chicago: Ferguson Publishing Co., 1969), p. 253.

Reflection

1. Which beatitude do I like best? Which one puzzles me most?
2. Jesus honors tradition. Is it possible to respect tradition in a society that is future oriented and impatient with history?
3. Do the high ideals of the Sermon on the Mount discourage me or liberate me?
4. Jesus commands us to respect the human dignity of each person. That is easy with persons I like. How could I see such dignity in people that repel me, those I hate and those I avoid?
5. Do I worship without having made an effort to be reconciled to people from whom I am estranged?
6. Have I tried loving my enemies?
7. Do I love only those who are nice to me?
8. Am I a contract person, demanding equal return for all the good I do for others?
9. Have I acquired a positive self-love as contrasted with a negative self-love which is selfishness?
10. How well do I appreciate that God's grace will be needed to respond to Christ's ideals in the Sermon on the Mount?

Prayer

Jesus, like a new Moses, you delivered a series of sayings that are meant to show me how to live the covenant of love with you, others and myself. You have gone beyond Moses by showing me the interior side of law. You challenge me to change my heart and my attitudes. You are thoughtful enough to know I cannot do this alone. I need you and the stream of loving grace to make it possible. Begin now to send me that amazing grace.

6 Do Piety Quietly

Sincere Religion (Mt. 6:1-18)

Hamlet says that "with devotion's visage, and pious action, we do sugar o'er the devil himself" (act 3, scene 1). There is nothing worse than a bad man pretending to be a saint. Everyone doubtless has a personal example of the public saint who is a devil at home. A comedian once said that one should beware of certain people on the day they receive Communion. It is an irreverent statement, to be sure, but comes painfully close to home.

Jesus was not against works of piety, but he knew the awful temptation to use piety as a cover up either for outright vice or for sterility of soul. He throws the searchlight not on the pious deed but on the intention behind the act. If it is your intention to be noticed, then do not do it. Are you looking for admiration, a public stroking? Forget it. Look for your strokes somewhere else.

Good works, gifts to charities and public praying should always be done with a sense of modesty and privacy. Look for approval from God. The warm feeling that comes from public acclaim in such matters vitiates the act, especially the good deeds to others. A novice once asked the dying St. Vincent de Paul to advise him of the best way to deal with the poor. His reply was to love them, so that they can forgive you for the bread you give them.

Piety's greatest pitfall is hypocrisy. It is a simple trap to fall into because the exterior act can so easily take on a life of its own. Hence, the more externalized the deed, the greater the possibility of the disappearance of the interior intention. What is worse yet, of course, is the fact that the general acceptance of the merit of good works affords malicious and unprincipled people the chance to look good while privately doing evil.

Works of piety need regular evaluation. The intention should be tested and the element of self-effacement examined. We should relax and perform our pious acts quietly.

Overcome Materialism (Mt. 6:19-34)

Pope John XXIII, born and raised a farmer, reminded us to love the soil. Though the work is hard and sometimes the return is little, you will find in the good earth and fields a sure refuge from dangerous materialism.

Note that he used the adjective dangerous. It implies the need for a balance in regard to the use and acquisition of material goods. In themselves they are not bad. God created earth and ". . . saw that it was good" (Gn. 1:25). The problem is what people do with the goods of the earth. If they approach them with avarice, they abuse the heritage. As a character in Chaucer's "Pardoner's Tale" says, "Avarice is the root of all evil."

Jesus does not speak of avarice frequently except in the "Lay not up . . . treasures" (Mt. 6:19-21) text in which he comments on misers, advising them to store up spiritual treasures instead. Rather, he dwells on the attitude of anxiety toward material goods.

He is not teaching irresponsibility and the lack of proper financial planning for the future, but is attacking the irrational fear that grips insecure people and causes them to fret and sometimes literally worry themselves to death. The prevalence of hypertension and the resultant strokes and heart attacks offer more than ample proof of the consequences of an over-anxious quest for material goods.

As Jesus notes, no one can add a single hour to life, but, in the final analysis, everyone can do a lot to shorten that life. The heart specialists, the tranquilizers at the drug stores, and the couches of the counselors testify to an anxious society that suffers for its unrestrained quests. W. H. Auden captured its spirit when he referred to it as the "Age of Anxiety."

To this anxious age Jesus speaks of the lilies of the field and the birds of the air. He knows perfectly well that we cannot imitate birds and plants. We can, however, see in them the meaning of God's abiding providence. Studies tell us much about the decline of faith and the rise of stress. There is a real connection. The loss of inner calm is partly due to a loss of faith and the childlike trust that should characterize kingdom persons. The meaning of the lilies of the field is not a mindless passivity before the divine gift, but an intelligent and trusting faith in the Lord.

Reflection

1. I know of some people who are terrific in public and terrible at home. How would I overcome such blindness were it true of me?
2. I am a regular church attender. What must I do to make my daily life correspond to my piety?
3. I dislike hypocrites. But what are the small or large hypocrisies of my own life?
4. Do I perform acts of piety in addition to going to Mass, such as saying the Rosary, reading the Bible, making the Stations?
5. Am I showy about my religious acts? Does my piety make me a smug Catholic?
6. Greed corrupts the rich, and sometimes even the poor. Avarice is the root of all evil. Are there traces of greed in my life?
7. What is my best defense against materialism?
8. What is the difference between prudent financial management and greed?
9. Why should I work just as hard in improving my attitudes as my behavior?
10. How can the Sermon on the Mount improve me as a person?

Prayer

My Lord Jesus, your preaching was effective because you witnessed what you said. I am more moved by witnesses than preachers. If I listen to preachers, it is because they are witnesses. Like you. With your example and power before me, I will strive to be a convinced Christian witness. Then, when I say something, my words will have the power of witness behind them. Without you, I cannot do this. With you, I will be an effective witness.

7   Curb Rash Criticism

Evaluate with Love (Mt. 7:1-6)

Obviously, intelligent people are supposed to use their reason and judgment. Jesus certainly does not intend to silence the critical faculty. Religion enjoyed a honeymoon period for a time when the believers rarely raised a dissenting voice. In fact, so passive were the faithful that wags often said that they were indeed like little lambs, to be prayed over and fleeced.

Inevitably, the worm turned and a torrent of dissent and criticism welled up within the church. Like everything else in life, some of it was good, some of it was overdone, and some of it was simply wrong. A few of the critics, who possessed the same ability to fail humanly as anyone else, were captivated by their own rhetoric and, instead of being helpful, became merely vocational crabs, with the result that their pronouncements resembled a sustained whine rather than an informed criticism that would be both a saving grace and a helpful contribution to the discussion.

Jesus says that we must not judge rashly lest we be subject to the same type of evaluation ourselves. It is similar to the Irish mother who might scold her dolt of a son, "Others will treat you the way you've treated me." Extremes do breed extremes and surely there was every reason to expect that passive lambs would one day rise and become howling dogs. Most institutions should expect no less and be strong enough both to improve where needed and to wait out the rest with some measure of humor.

Those overly captivated by their newly-found skill at criticizing should recall the Lord's words. The immediate special punishment reserved for them is the threat of becoming a lost generation, feeling virtuous in their negativism and hopelessly mired in a mind-set that needs ever-newer evils and follies to mourn lest their cups of tea do completely sour.

Pray Like a Believer (Mt. 7:7-11)

One of the notable occurrences in modern theology has been the development of the theology of hope. It is a happy antidote to the age of anxiety and the fashionable despair that weaves its distressing way through so much current drama, literature, films, and think pieces. The prevailing cynicism and despair of many intellectuals needs the salutary correction offered by the theology of hope.

Jesus is Lord. He has risen from the dead. He opens for us unlimited possibilities of personal, spiritual development. He does not eliminate tragedy. He reminds us that we also have a purifying cross to carry. The Lutheran minister Dietrich Bonhoeffer wrote about this from his jail cell before his death. He spoke of the need to avail ourselves of the costly grace in which discipleship, that is, the following of Jesus, will require tough choices and consequent struggles.

But he saw victory beyond the present sorrows. Hope in the promise of Christ is not misplaced. This is the framework in which Christ's words about prayer must be read. Prayer will be answered in the sense that the expectation Christ plants in our hearts will not be frustrated. What he promised he will deliver. Our asking and knocking are but specific forms of reaching out to the Lord for his continuous coming.

Tennyson appreciated the power of prayer when he placed these words, in *Idllys of the King*, on the lips of the dying King Arthur:

If thou shouldst never see my face again,
Pray for my soul. More things are wrought by prayer
Than this world dreams of. Wherefore, let they voice
Rise like a fountain for me night and day.
For what are men better than sheep or goats
That nourish a blind life within the brain,
If, knowing God, they lift not hands of prayer
Both for themselves and those who call them friends?

—Alfred Tennyson

Identify False Prophets (Mt. 7:15-23)

Times of crises are times of confusion. Because of the confusion people cry out for someone to rise up and clear the air. They look for messiahs and prophets. Recent history has been a trying time and the need for interpreters has been accelerated. And a great many "saviors" have arisen, often in sheep's clothing. But, as Jesus mentioned, we should be sure there is a sheep inside the sheepskin.

Happily, a great number of voices have been a blessing to everyone. Pope John Paul II has carried forward the task of preparing the church for the year 2000 when we celebrate two millennia of preaching the Gospel. Lay leaders, bishops and pastors across the world are quietly and energetically joined in this common effort to bring Christ to every corner of the earth.

Sadly, other voices have capitalized on the doom and, instead of preaching the Gospel (Good News), are intent on feeding us a constant diet of *Dysangel* (Bad News, a term used by Nietzsche) to further depress their listeners. They are sweet enough and, wearing their gentle sheepskin, they look harmless enough. But their nagging defeatism seems to beckon a faithlessness which does not compare with the real Gospel. We will know them by their fruits.

Their measure should be examined critically. If it leads to hopelessness, then it is not Gospel. Their personal performance also deserves scrutiny. A prophet, whether false or true, is a public figure and is subject to public review. In the words of a current expression, the public prophet must overcome his credibility gap.

Build on a Solid Foundation (Mt. 7:24-29)

The church's one foundation is Jesus Christ our Lord. The enormous growth of religious studies and thought in the past fifteen years makes Jesus' saying about building one's house on rock even more pertinent. The new theology, liturgical reforms, extensive developments in religious education, the wide expansion of biblical research and the thorough-going renewal of church structures all demand that the new growths be carefully aligned to the tree of Christ's grace. If these branches are not part of the true vine they will wither and die.

Unfortunately, it is not at all evident that all the new branches are indeed rooted in the one foundation of Christ. Too much has come too soon, and there must be a review and evaluation of all that has happened in order that we can more clearly see how it relates to a solid foundation. This is not to raise alarmist fears from the foundation. In fact, most of it is truly a genuine growth and breathes the authentic presence of the Lord.

The point is that such an astonishing abundance needs to be organized, synthesized, sorted out, and evaluated to make sure that it remains close to the sustaining and abiding power of Christ. We must not let the rootless style of modern life affect the depth of religion. Jesus advises us to build on rock and not on sand. It is an admonition that is most pertinent today.

Reflection

1. Do I love gossiping? Am I prone to rash judgement?
2. What do I think of the mother who said to her son, "Others will treat you the way you treated me"?
3. There was a time when a Catholic rarely criticized the church. Now it is a fashionable pastime. Where do I stand on such behavior?
4. Am I by temperament a negative thinker?
5. Do I pray with persistence and hope?
6. How do I treat people who seem to be self defeating, without hope and even justifying such a negative posture?
7. Do I believe in the power of prayer?
8. Have I noticed any false prophets in the church and society?
9. Why did Pope John XXIII advise us not to listen to the prophets of gloom?
10. While the church should be a loving community, why must it also have a strong and sound institutional structure? What happens to a church built on sand?

Prayer

My Lord and Judge, you have the divine perspective from which to evaluate human actions. My own vision is limited both by my experience and the roots of evil that beset me. I often rush to judgment and then regret my haste. I need your heavenly light to get a broader view of human relations. I want to be understanding and compassionate. Curb my rashness. Enlighten my judgements.

8, 9 Ten Miracles

The poet William Blake suggests that life progresses from innocence to experiences, and then to *organized* innocence. This insight could be of some use in understanding the miracles of Jesus. The innocent appreciation of the miracles is like a child's delight with a magician at a birthday party. The sheer wonder of the event enchants the observer.

But then experience manifests itself in a questioning attitude and a demand for meaning. The questioning probes the possibility and the reality of the miracles. What really happened? What is the message of the miracles? The demand for meaning tries to make sense out of the miracle and to see its application to personal life.

The level of organized innocence finds the believer once again recovering the simple acceptance of miracles, but with a difference. The perception and acceptance is enriched by the purification that resulted from the questioning and by the illumination arising from the efforts to find meaning in the miracles.

Today, the first two steps of Blake's insight generally pervade most Bible study groups. The innocents may tend to treat the miracles as though they were magic occurrences. The experientialists tend almost to dismiss the miracles as happening at all. Instead, they concentrate on the meaning of the miracle story. Among them, some would say, "It doesn't matter what happened. It's the meaning that counts." In reply, the disillusioned innocents fight back, declaring, "It does matter what happened, regardless of the meaning." Even so, the innocents also speak of meaning, usually in terms of miracles as proofs of Christ's divinity.

These discussions are part of a growth period toward Blake's third suggested stage: organized innocence. In it one is born again, becomes once more the little child and recovers the sense of wonder. He notices both life's many mysteries and the unique disclosures of those mysteries in the miracles of Jesus. The danger of the first stage, the stage of innocence, is that the believer may remain fixated on a mindless view of miracles. The danger of the second, the stage of experience, is that he may tend to discount even the possibility of miracles. Far from being mindless, the experientialist may become too mind-full and see only what scientific observation seems to allow.

Matthew tells the ten miracle stories of chapters 8 and 9 from the viewpoint of an organized innocent, announcing their reality with straightforward conviction, yet also surrounding them with meaning. He describes them as transparent events illustrating the victory of Christ's kingdom over the evil one. Matthew's selection of ten miracles in itself possesses a meaning. He evokes the memory of the ten miracle plagues of the Old Testament when God won a victory for the people against the evil power of the Pharaoh. The plague stories were the narrative of a particular onslaught of God against one example of the world's injustice and evil. Matthew says that the miracles of Jesus are a universal attack by the kingdom of God against all the world's evil. The particular victory along the banks of the Nile foreshadows the universal victory of Jesus along the banks of the Jordan.

Matthew sees the miracles of Jesus in terms of what he is *doing*, not so much in terms of what he *is*. It is possible, however, to go further and make inferences from Christ's deeds in order to achieve an understanding of his personhood and nature. To Matthew, there is even more meaning in the miracle stories than the battle of good and evil. Important though it is, that battle may seem too abstract and too difficult to grasp. Matthew, however, also stresses its *personal* meaning. In our own age, which prefers the personalized approach, this may seem more relevant.

There is a clue in the fact that nine of the ten miracles are healing. This is to show that the Good News of the kingdom is more than a beautiful idea. The kingdom takes concrete shape in the healing compassion of Jesus. Christ's words are Gospel. So are his deeds. Miracles are the nonverbal counterpart of Gospel proclamation and the healings, the body talk of the evangelical mission.

There is a renewed interest today in the ministry of healing, a rediscovery of its role in preaching the Good News. Many hospitals are beginning to welcome the religious healing ministry to complete their therapeutic program, and the work of the chaplain is assuming a new richness. Doctors, psychologists, psychiatrists, and clinical pastoral ministers are in many instances undertaking coordinated healing efforts. Such a team effort rescues the spiritual healer from an unwarranted religious fundamentalism which does not acknowledge the expertise of the medical profession. It also widens the consciousness of the medical profession insofar as the spiritual mystery of the patients. The pitfalls of both religious and medical fundamentalism are hereby avoided and the patient is the richer for having a wider response to his needs.

The miracle stories of Matthew thus call attention to several discussions central to our time: (1) the reality of miracles; (2) the meaning of miracles; and, (3) the relationship of the healing ministry to the full task of healing.

Popular belief in the reality of miracles endures to this day. Among Catholics, miracle shrines such as those at Lourdes, Guadalupe and Fatima attract a continual stream of devout believers. The canonization process of the Catholic Church requires a set number of certified miracles before the person is declared a saint.

The miracles of the Bible come in three forms: healings, resurrections and nature-wonders. The ten miracles that we are considering contain these three forms. There are eight healing stories (leper, centurion's servant, Peter's mother-in-law, possessed persons, paralytic, lady with the bleeding, two blind men, the mute); one resurrection (Jairus' daughter); and one nature-wonder (calming of the storm). Critical examination of these miracle stories (experientialist stage) raises questions about their being examples of a special divine intervention. It is possible to say that the healings are psychosomatic cures in which the awakening of religious faith sets in motion the processes that lead to healing. This line of argument would also apply to the raising of the daughter of Jairus. It is possible that she was in a death-like coma from which she was aroused by subconscious suggestion.

However, in John's Gospel, the Lazarus story raises special problems if one is looking for psychosomatic solutions. His body had begun to decompose after four days in the grave which scarcely left much room for such a solution. An alternate interpretation has emerged. It proposes that the Lazarus story is a fictional dramatic homily created for funeral liturgies in the apostolic church. Thus, it becomes a symbolic story intended to illustrate the belief in immortality.

The nature wonders elicit little acknowledgement of credibility from the questioners. Perhaps the sea was not calmed. Perhaps the branch of the fig tree did not wither. Perhaps these are action parables. In other words, perhaps they too are invented stories intended to dramatize the meaning of Christ's mission and destiny. He is Lord of nature and history. If that idea is too abstract, why not illustrate it with sea calmings and branch witherings?

What prompts such questioning? Critics are, quite rightly, anxious to purify religious belief from any attachment to a magic mentality. They wish to preserve the cherished values of the human and natural, and strive to conserve the role of the human in human life to avoid a concept of divine action in human affairs that leaves little room for human initiative. An overemphasis on the divine would keep believers in a stage of childhood, an innocence that never has an opportunity to mature.

There clearly is a real need for the speculation of the critics. They contribute to the maturing of the believers' judgments. However, the speculations themselves require review and evaluation. It would be as childish to accept a speculation uncritically as to approach a miracle story naively. The mere claim that such and such a miracle is a fanciful invention does not necessarily mean that it is.

The critical approach that the Catholic Church takes toward such postbiblical miracles as those at the shrines and those proposed in canonization processes is instructive. These innocent announcements are subjected to extensive, often tedious, experiential tests. The insights of both empirical science and faith are brought to bear in canonization cases. Morris West's *Devil's Advocate* assembles a folio of data in an effort to discredit the miracle. He offers speculations designed to give it a purely human interpretation.

But the saint's advocate also speaks and, out of this give and take, this interaction of faith and reason, this exchange between human and the divine, a resolution slowly emerges. Some miracles pass the test; others do not. Processes similar to such advocacies are applied in the examination of miracles in such places as Lourdes.

In a sense, the miracles of the New Testament are new for each generation of believers. The scientific mind automatically raises questions. Are these miracles only psychosomatic? What about the resurrections? Are the nature-wonders only metaphors created to put across a point?

It is conceivable that nature-wonders are all mere parables or that they are more real than that. The questioning attitude does not necessarily lead to reducing all miracles to some kind of human oc-currence or invention. Healings, resurrections and nature-wonders are quite conceivable as miracle events with an historical basis.

All of these observations may seem tedious to innocent believers and even contentious to experiential believers. They are in fact important elements in the process of faith-knowing. Not everyone will pursue the speculative paths described here. Each in-dividual must find his or her own way to mature in faith-knowing. The important thing is that an ascent to mature faith-knowing does occur. A community of organized innocents is to be preferred to something less.

Obviously, the route to this maturing is not simply through the in-vestigation of Matthew's miracle stories. Much more is at stake. The recurrence of Matthew's dominant theme—conversion to the kingdom of God—is a far more comprehensive goal for faith development. The miracle stories happen to be both a relevant and a dramatic peg upon which to hang this particular discussion.

While the above discussion of miracles has its particular per-tinence, a few special comments on the miracles themselves also seems in order.

Each miracle story possesses one detail, one human interest item, that adds up to a tapestry of values.

Leper (8:1-4). Jesus tells the leper to show his cleansed body to the priest as Jewish law requires. This indicates that Christ en-couraged official church review of the reality of the miracle occurren-ces, even as occurs today.

Centurion (8:5-13). The centurion displays not only an attractive modesty and self-effacing humility, but also a maturity of faith per-ception. He knows Christ can cure without magical touches. Jesus admires and praises this self-deprecating man and the maturity of his faith. It is good to recall that this soldier's faith-full prayer, "O Lord, I am not worthy," is always heard at Holy Communion.

Curing Peter's Mother-in-law (8:14-15). The cure of Peter's mother-in-law offers a domestic touch. With her fever gone, she can resume her household duties. And, given the age-old existence of in-law antipathies, it is pleasant to find that Peter appears to have resolved that impasse in human relations.

Calming the Storm (8:23-37). The calming of the storm is as important for the storm as for the calming. When Jesus tells the apostles that they have little faith, he is pointing out that people of great faith realize that mature living will involve plenty of rough waters. Christ may seem asleep when we are in deep trouble. He is, in reality, very much with us and expects us to do as much as we can to weather the storms of life. Rough seas are not signs of God's absence but rather personal challenges to forge ahead, never losing faith in Christ.

The Exorcism (8:28-34). With the revival of the occult and the popular interest in exorcism, the story of driving the devils out of two possessed men into a pack of swine acquires a new relevance. It is clearly a confrontation of the kingdom of God with the kingdom of evil. Christ's attack on evil spirits is one more stage in his process of vanquishing the prince of darkness. For obvious reasons, Jesus did not meet with much welcome from the pig raisers of the neighborhood who were less interested in religious victories when the victory imperiled their own economic futures.

Paralytic (9:1-8). The cure of the paralytic brings up a very old idea that some day may come back into its own. Biblical people believed that there was a link between sin and sickness. Jesus first forgives the sins of the paralytic and only then cures his paralysis. The people are scandalized at Christ's presuming to forgive sins. Only God could do that. This expression, which appears so often in the New Testament, has two sources in the Old Testament. God frequently addresses Ezekiel as "Son of Man." The usage in this case involves the humanity of the prophet, a humanity prone to sin. The other source is in Daniel, chapter seven, where there is a vision of a Son of Man coming in the clouds of heaven to bring justice and judgement to the world:

As the visions during the night continued, I saw
One like a son of man coming,
On the clouds of heaven;
He received dominion, glory and kingship;
That shall not be taken away,
His kingship shall not be destroyed.

—Dn. 7:13-14

When Jesus calls himself the Son of Man he is combining the humanity idea of Ezekiel with the messianic figure in Daniel. He claims brotherhood in our humanity—in everything except sin. He also discloses his messianic destiny, the destiny of one who shall have dominion over all. That conquest includes both evil and the sickness and death that are its visible sign.

The people of biblical times were quicker than we are to associate sin and sickness. They seemed to see a link between spiritual illness (sin) and physical illness. Psychology's insights into psychosomatic illness may open the way to a recovery of the biblical view of spiritual-somatic illness. It is an idea that may be worth considering.

The Daughter of Jairus (9:18-26). The importance of resurrection stories in the gospels is to foreshadow the central message of Christianity, the death and resurrection of Jesus. The detail of the keening mourners is intended simply to stress the realism of the situation.

The Bleeding Lady (9:20-21). The appealing aspect of this story lies in the fact the lady is too shy to approach Jesus. She is convinced that if she can secretly touch the hem of his cloak, that will be enough. She resembles those who today, in quiet piety, keep pieces of cloth that once touched the bodies of saints. Luke enriches the story by having Jesus ask who touched him, for he felt power going out from him (Lk. 8:40-56). The woman is brought forward, testifies to her twelve-year-long bleeding illness and leaves the scene cured.

Two Blind Men (9:27-31). In almost all the miracle stories something is said about the faith of the cured. This faith includes both a trust in Christ and an awareness of his power to cure. Jesus asks the blind men if they really believe he can cure them. They say, "Yes, Lord." Then they see. Jesus asks them not to tell anyone. But how could they keep such Good News/Gospel to themselves?

Exorcising a Mute (9:32-34). This tenth miracle, the second exorcism, increases the admiration of the people. It also causes a growing anger on the part of the religious officials that shows that miracles of themselves do not necessarily prove to the witnesses the appearance of God's work and kingdom. The people and the religious officials saw the same wonders. The people sensed a divine wonder. The officials termed what had occurred, occult and devilish works: "By the prince of devils he casts out devils."

The miracle stirs faith if the observer is open to the possibility. By contrast, it seems to stir disbelief in those who refuse to see. That is why John's Gospel speaks of miracles as signs of judgment which separate those who believe from those who do not.

The ten miracles present a tapestry of values and possibilities: (1) submit miracles to official church review; (2) move beyond the magical mentality as the centurion did; (3) retain their simple domestic value; (4) expect your measure of stormy existence, believing Christ is with you; (5) allow for exorcism; (6) ponder the possibility of spiritual-somatic illness; (7) affirm your belief in your resurrection; (8) if you are shy, then touch the hem; (9) recall who faith is the central component in miracles; and, (10) do not forget, miracles do not always produce belief in the observers.

Reflection

1. The poet William Blake says I progress from innocence to experience to organized innocence. Which stage am I in?
2. In general, how do miracle stories affect me?
3. What helps me to have a sense of wonder?
4. Who finds it harder to have a sense of wonder, a man or a woman?
5. What does it mean to say that Matthew approaches miracles from the viewpoint of an organized innocent?
6. What Old Testament experience does Matthew's account of the ten miracles of Jesus recall?
7. How does Matthew show the miracles as a form of Christ's battle with evil?
8. Nine of these ten miracles deal with healing. What does that tell me about Jesus?
9. What does a spiritual healing ministry say to the medical profession?

10. What does the medical profession say to the spiritual healing ministry?
11. What evidence do I have that some of today's Protestants believe in miracles?
12. What evidence do I have that Catholics believe miracles happen today?
13. What are the three kinds of miracles I find in the Gospels?
14. In a canonization process, what does the "devil's advocate" do regarding the miracles performed by the proposed saint's intercession?
15. How do I feel about critical approaches to the miracle stories of the Bible? Does this weaken my faith? Can it make me stronger in my beliefs?
16. What does the calming of the storm at sea have to say about the trials that will come in my faith life?
17. Why does Jesus apply the "Son of Man" theme to himself? How does the expression apply both to his humanity and his messiahship?
18. Psychology sometimes links emotional disturbance with a physical illness. This is a psychosomatic illness. Can there also be a sin-related illness, a religio-somatic sickness?
19. The "bleeding lady" touched the hem of Christ's robe in faith and was healed. Is this not like the devout who touch the relics of saints in faith, hoping to be healed?
20. If I saw or experienced a miracle, would it automatically increase my faith?

Prayer

Lord of all life and nature, your power sustains all that exists. There are times when I need various kinds of healing — physical, emotional and spiritual. I know you will always heal me from sin when I am open to reconciliation with you, myself and others. I can sometimes hope for emotional and physical healings, but must realize that these healings must be ordered to spiritual wholeness. I trust in your wisdom in this regard. I ask always for the faith that will make me whole and holy.

10 Training Apostles

Matthew 10 concentrates on the question of leadership. Jesus knows that he must create leaders out of the twelve men he has chosen to give form to his vision. Leadership involves a goal and a plan. The goal is not enough; a plan is necessary to make sure that it can be reached.

Jesus begins with the goal: Evangelize the believers. Evangelization means preaching conversion from sin to grace, from darkness to light of the kingdom of heaven. The term "heaven" is used instead of "God" because the Hebrew reverence for the holy Name demanded that it rarely be spoken.

The Lord insists that the first goal is the evangelization of believers. The first missionary proclamation is not to nonbelievers, pagans, moon-adoring Babylonians or sun-worshipping Egyptians. Tell the Good News to the believers first. Physician, cure thyself. Present the Gospel to the believers and then bring it to all nations. Perform this evangelical preaching in both word and deed. Match lip talk with body talk. Speak of the Good News, but accompany that speech with works of healing and exorcism. These deeds of compassion are nonverbal proclamations of the Gospel.

In the first covenant, God spoke to Israel the Ten Words (Ten Commandments) and accompanied those words with the marvelous works of manna, quail and the healings with the bronze serpent. Now, in the second covenant, the public preaching is accompanied by public acts of love. The goal is a total ministry, to the believers first, but eventually to all people.

This evangelical technique will be the standard missionary approach used by St. Paul, initially to the believers and then to the gentiles. Evangelization will be equally successful today if the same strategy is employed. The community of believers needs a fresh evangelization, a renewed conversion, as it undertakes a contemporary proclamation of the Gospel to the world.

Evangelization is the goal. What is the plan?

Jesus offers his apostles four steps: (1) travel light; (2) do not forget the human; (3) prepare to suffer; and, (4) sense the divine presence. In advising his leaders to travel light, he teaches the need for singlemindedness in pursuit of the goal. Material possessions and concerns distract one from the all-consuming purpose of the Gospel. Freedom from unnecessary ownership means freedom for total dedication to the goal. The church has not forgotten this ideal. The vow of poverty espoused by the religious orders, its articulation in the dream of St. Francis, its inspiring appearance in the great missionary congregations and its newest and compelling evocation in the community of Mother Teresa of India illustrate the enduring witness to the Lord's desire.

Success in evangelization will thus demand a shedding of worldly concerns by the evangelizers. Leaders who wish to place their lives at the service of the Gospel must begin by making a firm decision to eliminate from their concerns anything that would distract them from the one thing necessary, the announcing of Jesus and his salvation. Only attachment to the Lord will work. Any other involvement will dilute the unflagging attention that in the past has so surely opened the heart of people to Christ and will do so again when the same clear consecration is present.

Jesus is not training angels, but people. Hence he is insistent that his leaders remember that they are dealing with humans: He instructs us that when we enter a home, bless it (verse 12). Other translations have him asking the apostles to say *shalom* (peace) as they enter a home, with the intention that the blessing will create an atmosphere of trust.

Presenting the Gospel is not to be an adversary proceeding. Although the kingdom of heaven is against the kingdom of evil, there is no need to start the conversation in a mood of hostility. As convert-makers of former days knew so well: you may win the argument but lose a soul. It is necessary to create a sense of trust before any dialogue can begin. Say, "Peace to this house." In recent years, psychology began to operate on the same wavelength. Transactional analysis quite rightly claims that human involvements will get off to a better start when the participants can begin with an I'm OK — You're OK act of trust.

If this attitude of shalom is not present, there is little likelihood of openmindedness on the part of the hearers. The evangelist must help people to listen to the word of Christ. What point is there in antagonizing the listeners so that all their genes say no even before the Good News is heard. As any good lawyer or salesman knows, the yes factor in the customer and client must be addressed from the beginning.

Jesus teaches that you must be clever as snakes and innocent as doves (verse 16). The cunning of the serpent and the ingenuousness of the dove simply indicate that the evangelist should act intelligently, keeping in mind the psychology of the person addressed. Obviously, this does not call for cheating the hearer or tricking him or her into accepting Christ. Nothing could be farther from the spirit of Christ than engineering conversions. It simply means treating people as people. One should begin with peace, not with threats.

Some people inevitably will reject the message no matter how convincingly it is presented with trust beginnings and faith conviction. Again, Jesus offers the realistic evaluation: Shake the dust from your feet and go elsewhere. Give the listeners an adequate chance for conversion. When there is no hope for acceptance, give other people a chance. Travel light. Act humanly. Now, prepare for pain. Jesus leaves his potential leaders under no illusions. They must get ready to suffer and even to die for the kingdom. It will not be abstract suffering. It will involve a breaking away from family and from the comforts of domestic happiness. It involves the possibilities of arrest, jails, trials, beatings, and humiliations; not just the psychological pain of disappointment, but the social and physical brutalities of prisons, courts and whipping posts. Above all, the ultimate suffering these leaders can count as a possibility is martyrdom, death for love. The cost of discipleship will be high. Martyrdom may not be a certainty for all of them—apparently it was not for John—but it is the gamble Jesus asks them to make. To die for love, which is the essence of the kingdom, is a possibility for which they must be prepared.

All great religious leaders have faced up to and, in many instances, endured the possibilities of suffering and martyrdom. Today's bearers of the Gospel, if they hope to be effective, will need to accept them in advance. It is a costly discipleship to embrace, but courage of this high order is the hallmark of the religious leader who presumes to call people to Christ. Such leaders march forth to their task under the sign of the cross. They can expect no less.

They bring not peace but the sword. This is not a contradiction of what has been stated above about establishing a peaceful, trust beginning. The peaceful start is simply to make people aware of the tensions involved in pitting the kingdom of heaven against the kingdom of evil. It is to show them the dimensions of the moral drama. The sword refers to the determination of Jesus to conquer evil. The cross, with its element of suffering and death, shows the extent to which one will be called to face down evil and establish the kingdom.

No leader will walk alone. Jesus assures his apostles that nothing less than the divine power of the Spirit will be available to permit the heroic possibilities he envisions. The fearful, stuttering fishermen will be astonished to find themselves speaking bravely and articulately to judges, kings and wild mobs. Their words will rise up from the interior Spirit who will give them boldness when they need it.

The final step of the plan is to sense the divine presence. Jesus asks his leaders to treat the listeners in a human way, but he adds that it must all be done in a divine milieu or, as the medieval religious writers put it, under the aspect of eternity.

Apostolic leaders see the world as faith-knowers. Their world is charged with the grandeur of God. When they preach with faith, it is Christ who is heard. When the cup of water is given in his name, it is given to him. Contemporary language calls this a Christ mysticism. No matter what the terminology is, the reality remains the same. To be an evangelizer means to live and move and have one's being in Jesus; to sense the divine presence as the very air in which the whole evangelical project is carried out.

Augustine once wrote that a person who has faith believes in the word of God what he does not see, and his reward is to see and enjoy what he believes. This is the training and reward implied by Christ's words in Matthew 10.

Reflection

1. What do I understand by the term *evangelization*?
2. Why did not Jesus send the Apostles first to evangelize the moon--adoring Babylonians and the sun-worshiping Egyptians? Why did Jesus first evangelize the Jewish people?
3. Why should a missionary "travel light?"
4. If I am inviting an inactive Catholic back to church, or inviting an unchurched person to join my parish, what could I learn from Christ's words about imparting a peace and blessing upon entering a house?
5. How can I be clever as a snake and innocent as a dove? Is not this a contradictory position?
6. Should I anticipate disappointment when I share my faith with others? What are modern examples of people suffering pain and even death for sharing and living up to their faith in Christ?
7. Am I completely alone when I share my faith with others?
8. Is evangelization only a human act? Or only a divine act?
9. Do I know of many Catholics who do not wish to share their faith with others? Why does this happen?
10. Does my baptism have anything to do with my responsibility to share my faith with others?

Prayer

Evangelizing Lord, I would never have come to faith if you had not reached out to call Apostles to carry on your mission. If they had not in turn appointed bishops and others to evangelize, I would not have heard the word of conversion. Help me to share my faith so that this gift of salvation may be enjoyed by many others.

11   Jesus and Cousin John

John as the New Elijah (Mt. 11:1-19)

In a poem entitled "The Quickening of John the Baptist,"
Thomas Merton meditates on John's first meeting with Jesus in their
prenatal sanctuaries. John moves with Joy.

Sing in your cell, small anchorite!
How did you see in the eyeless dark?
What secret syllable
Woke your young faith to the mad truth
That an unborn baby could be washed in the Spirit of God?
You need no eloquence, wild bairn,
Your ecstacy is your apostolate.

—Thomas Merton

In the room of Elizabeth's womb, John experienced the burning
joy of Christ. Now, in Herod's prison, he calls out again to his cousin
Jesus for a reaffirmation of that hope that began so long ago. The
once wordless hope now is framed in the anxious question, "Are
thou he who is to come, or do we look for another?" (verse 3).

Jesus replies in terms of the signs of the divine presence among
men. The healings, which form the nonverbal counterpart of the
evangelical ministry, are offered to John as testimony. They are not
proofs of the divine presence in the rational, empirical sense; they require the sensitivity of faith to see that they represent the divine
milieu.

Jesus appears confident that John will understand his reply:
"Blest is the man who finds no stumbling block in me" (verse 6).
Many have seen the signs and have not detected the Spirit at work. If
the light of reason were all that was needed, then everyone would be
converted. These cures were the evidence of things that appear not
and the substance of that which is to be hoped for.

Such signs and wonders puzzle those who lack the depth that faith knowing can provide. Jesus proceeds to enlighten the people who are blind about what is going on. He begins with a glowing tribute to his cousin John and then comments on the childishness of the people and the stubbornness of the towns most favored by the signs and wonders. He begins with an evaluation of the people who belonged to the Baptist's cult during his spiritual crusades by the Jordan and in the desert. They obviously did not go out to hear a wishy-washy speaker nor a striking desert monarch. They somehow sensed that John was a prophet, the first one that the people had heard of in over four hundred years. They knew he was a real prophet, very much like the fiery Elijah from the middle ages of their history.

Elijah traveled light, ate the simple foods of nature, fought his way to the thrones of kings and bore the aura of the glory of God around him. Fearless in denouncing public evils, he smote consciences of high and low, performed signs and wonders (wondrous food for the widow of Zarephatha, consuming fire for the true sacrifice), and left an enduring impact on the consciousness of the community of believers.

The spirit of Elijah obviously appeared again in the person of John the Baptist. His presence reminded everyone that the kingdom of God required violence and that only the violent could take it. These seem strange words for those who see nonviolence as the religious ideal. But the violence in question is not physical brutality, but rather the strength of character needed to meet the demands of the kingdom. Believers are not called to torture anyone or to think it their noble mission to press anyone into the faith by force. If brutality occurs at all it is in the cross borne and courageously accepted by the believer.

It is the very mystery of the Holy Martyr that may be at stake in this discussion. This does not, of course, absolve the religious preacher from making demanding challenges on the spiritually corrupt, the morally bankrupt, or the blindly complacent of any age. Thus did Elijah face down the royal thrones of Ahab and Jezebel. Thus also did the Baptist confront those who came to hear his message in the desert.

Jesus pays his cousin an ultimate compliment when he said that never in history to this time had there been seen a man born of woman greater than John the Baptizer (verse 11). John's wise heart burst with love as he spurned his own life and laid it down for the sake of the kingdom when he denounced the moral corruption of Herod and his presumed wife. Not that John was unwilling to negotiate, discuss and attempt to convert and change the immoral hearts of his captors. However, once it was clear that they were unwilling to change, he chose the law of the kingdom and explicitly named their sin, a theme that occurs again in the story of John's martyrdom.

Jesus then turns the conversation to the fickleness of people. Nothing will satisfy them, neither the ascetic behavior of John nor the effort of Jesus to try the so-called human approach. Too many of the listeners were too childish. They acted as if it were all a game, like children playing at funerals and feasts: "We piped you a tune and you did not dance. We sang you a dirge and you did not wail" (verse 17).

Much of the crowd's reaction was that of an immature audience. Religion has both its ascetic side and its element of celebration. Fast and feast are two of its aspects. But by reducing them to the level of gaming, Jesus' listeners made a mockery of religion, treating it as a series of clever diversions from the ennui they were trying to escape. In their silliness they could not appreciate the depth of either fast or feast. Their religion was one of fads, for their faith had grown cold and their adulthood was arrested to a point where they missed the whole message of John and Jesus.

Failure to Repent (Mt. 11:20-30)

With the anger of an Elijah-like prophet, Jesus plainly denounced the most favored cities who had known the richness of the kingdom's signs and showed scarcely any interest in the divine love showered upon them. The Gospel, both preached and performed in Chorazin, Bethsaida and Capernaum, fell upon the stoniest ground. They loved the diversion but hated the message. And they were the supposed communities of faith, the blessed. They, presumably, were the centers of hope for the possibilities of belief.

Jesus hurled his judgments upon them. He had given them enough understanding and acceptance. He told them unequivocally that they would be more harshly treated than the admittedly sinful Sodom and the unbelieving Tyre and Sidon.

Of those to whom much is given, much is expected. God had lavished grace on the "big three" cities. Their ungrateful response was a rejection of the kingdom. That kingdom subsequently would charm an empire and influence the course of Western civilization. But Chorazin, Bethsaida and Capernaum would miss the incomparable beauty and lapse into darkness. Offered the wine, they chose less than water and became an enduring example of missed opportunity.

Clearly, the kingdom will be hidden from the so-called wise and prudent and revealed to the "merest children" (verse 25). The wise and prudent are those who rest on their own worldly wisdom. They are the sophisticated who are paralyzed by their own cleverness. They never understand that reason is God's gift for scanning the stars and reaching for the infinite. They seem not to know that reason is their god given talent to send forth ultimate questions to the shrine of holiness. It is not that such strivings will produce the kingdom, but that they open the heart to the unimagined miracle of grace which occurs when God responds to honest searching.

The merest children are not childish adults but mature people who have the humility to realize they do not know everything. They are the ones who have the extra perception, who wait with hearts turned toward skies they do not always understand. They are enchanted by the mystery of life and resist the temptation to reduce everything to some form of the here and now. This can be particularly difficult today when so much of life involves an attempt to process the information overload that pours into the human consciousness. Since even the best computer balks at the volume of data, it is small wonder that unmechanical thinkers and lovers will throw up their hands in anger and despair over the efforts to mesmerize and imprison them in the fruitless pursuit of imagining that data is everything.

There is comfort in the stars whether on a summer night or a cold winter evening. We journey to Europe and Asia to see Gothic cathedrals and Buddhist temples. These centers of religion are monuments to the human openness to the beyond. The stars, God's cathedrals, remind us of the need for a spiritual search beyond our endless tinkering and tampering with the world left to us as a heritage.

Christ's plain speech to the childish of his time, to the heartless cities, remains the biting rebuke it was on the shores of Galilee. We have our own versions of immaturity and insensitivity. The kingdom is still here, waiting to break through. The challenge is to stop playing games and grow up to the remarkable hope so close to our grasp and so sweet and refreshing. "Come to me, all you who are weary and find life burdensome. I will refresh you" (verse 28).

Reflection

1. The imprisoned Baptist needs his faith reaffirmed in Christ as messiah. Do I need my faith reaffirmed?
2. Jesus assures John by the witness of his signs and wonders. Is my faith strengthened by the Christian witness of others?
3. How was John the Baptist like Elijah?
4. What did Jesus mean by the "violence" needed to advance the Kingdom? Is not violence against Christ's message of peace?
5. What does Christ's judgment against favored cities in contrast with sinful ones mean for me?
6. If God has lavished his love and grace on me, will he not also expect more from me?
7. If I give my children a better education than I had, should I not expect better performance from them?
8. Why would the kingdom be denied to the wise and prudent and given to the merest children?
9. Jesus appeals to the child in me. What would be the difference between being childish and childlike?
10. Do some people never grow up in their religion?

Prayer

Jesus, you call me simultaneously to be a maturing adult and a childlike person. Sometimes I feel I want to be the "master of the universe" and be in total charge of my life and others. I know I must learn to face the mystery of life and your mystery. For that I need to let go, let be and let grow. Show me how to do this.

12 Tensions

Basic tensions underlie all of life and none are so persistent as those that involve the opposing demands of law and freedom. The two Sabbath stories in this chapter illustrate those tensions. In the first, the apostles pick some corn to relieve their hunger—but such harvesting was forbidden by law on the sabbath. In the second, Jesus cures on the sabbath. The objection is that doctoring is forbidden. In both cases Jesus provides examples of exceptions to the law that favored the demands of persons. King David ate the Holy Bread in the temple on the sabbath when he was hungry. Priests could work in the temple on the Sabbath without breaking the work law. Who would not rescue a trapped animal on the Sabbath if it was necessary? And, if an animal could be saved, why couldn't a person be helped who is more important?

Jesus points out to the legalists that they have denied the basic tensions of life. They should know that law and freedom, rule and person, are two sides of a coin and must be kept in balance if a mature view is to be maintained. Jesus obeyed the law, but he also saw to the needs of persons. It is not a question of either/or. There must be freedom and there must be law.

Freedom without law is anarchy: Doing your own thing. Law without freedom is totalitarianism: A mechanical bending of people to abstract demands. Laws are made to serve persons, not persons to be the servants of the law. The Sabbath was made for people, not people for the Sabbath. What Jesus is indicating is that the basic tension of life is resolved not by abolishing it but by taking hold of it and using it wisely to serve the needs of the maturing person. One does not eliminate the tension by preferring one pole over the other, but rather should take hold of both poles and face the richer life that will be the consequence.

With this dialogue on tension, Matthew introduces the first notes of opposition to the kingdom. No longer are the works and words of Jesus seen as Good News by all. The comfortably religious are getting worried. They are beginning to realize that Jesus is really confronting their way of life and they do not like it. He is not merely a newly eloquent rabbi. He is a dangerous person, tampering, as they see it, with the sacredness of their traditions.

They accuse him of being a sorcerer. His ability to cast out devils is not a sign of God's kingdom but a form of diabolical magic. With the simplest of logic, Jesus asks them why the devil would give him the power to get rid of devils. It does not make sense. Successful corporations do not dissolve themselves. Secure citizens would hardly be expected to go into exile. Conquerors do not normally give up the territory they possess. The devil is not going to give up his trophies. But their minds were made up. Jesus was not going to confuse them with facts. Logic works when there is trust which serves as a basis for discourse. They did not trust Jesus and no effort on his part seemed likely to establish the *shalom* that would help them to see the beauty of the gift he was offering.

Reflection

1. Jesus frequently asks me to focus on the centrality of human dignity. Do I tend to overlook the person before me?
2. Rules are meant to serve and protect people. Do I use rules to get my way or exploit people?
3. Do I ever feel the tension between freedom and law, between the needs of the person and the requirements of the law?
4. What happens when we have freedom and no law?
5. What is the result of law and no freedom?
6. Would I be better off honoring the needs of a person and forgetting the rules of life and society altogether?
7. Jesus begins to experience opposition to his person and teaching. Could I experience opposition to my faith witness?
8. What is blasphemy against the Holy Spirit (Mt. 12:31-32)?
9. How does the Jonah story prefigure Easter?
10. Why do people resist and refuse love, no matter how generously and selflessly it is offered to them?

Prayer

My Lord, every day I meet many people and deal with many regulations and rules, whether those of the household or in the workplace. I try to keep my balance, respecting the needs of persons and following the rules that protect and serve us all. I admit that I frequently lose my way and fail to hit the balance. Sometimes I hurt people. Sometimes I misuse rules. No one wins. You are Eternal Wisdom. Make me wise, loving and law-abiding.

13 Parables: Stories of the Kingdom

Matthew records ten major parables of Jesus:
The Sower: 13:3-23
The Weeds: 13:26-30
Mustard Seed: 13:31-32
Leaven: 13:33
The Pearl: 13:44-46
The Net: 13:47-50
Lost Sheep: 18:10-14
Grape Pickers: 19:30—20:16
The Vineyard: 21: 33-46
The Wedding Feast: 22:1-14

Taken together, these stories encompass the meaning of the church. They speak of preachers, congregations, processes of growth, values, sinners, ranges of devotion, martyrdom, and ecstacy. In one way or another they provide unforgettable insights into the spiritual nature of the church and offer models for understanding what it ought to be. They are not the only examples, but they do touch upon many of the central bases of the meaning of the church/kingdom.

The Second Vatican Council devoted close attention to expanding the appreciation of the church to models beyond the organizational one. Prior to it the widespread emphasis on the church as Christ's Mystical Body did much to divert attention from a narrow, sometimes exclusive, concentration on institutional details. The document on the church, *Lumen Gentium*[*] (Light of Nations), placed in the forefront the model of the church as a spiritual mystery and a com-

[*]*Vatican Council II: The Conciliar and Post Conciliar Documents*, Austin Flannery, Gen. ed. (Northport: N.Y.: Costello Publishing Co., 1975).

munity of believers (people of God). Matthew's ten parables of the kingdom all shed light on these themes of mystery and people.

The Sower (Mt. 13:1-23)

In the parable of the sower Jesus demonstrates that evangelization will need to face a range of consciousness all the way from the most militant resistance to the most enthusiastic openness. We have already seen this totally resistant strain in the story of the blasphemers of the Holy Spirit, the advocates of antifaith.

This is the first of the four stages of response to evangelization in the parable of the sower. One way of characterizing the remaining three stages is in terms of thrill-seekers, compromisers, and the truly open. Because religion offers ecstacy and the ultimate peaks of spiritual happiness, it is a natural mecca for thrill-seekers. While there is nothing wrong in itself in seeking a kick out of life, something is amiss when that becomes a way of life.

Those whose only interest in religion is an emotional high are doomed to disappointment. Religion is a mixture of comfort and affliction, just as life is. It leads people from the first joys into long-term ordinariness and a fair amount of aridity. For Israel, the exultant crossing of the Red Sea was followed by the forty years of pilgrimage through the desert. Those crossing the river of joy into the kingdom can expect the rough hewn pilgrimage characteristic of many years of persistent disciplined living.

Plant the evangelical seed into the consciousness of a faddish thrill-seeker and await the inevitable death of that tender seed. That audience is too superficial. It will go on to some other kind of high. "Part of it fell on rocky ground, where it had little soil. It sprouted at once, since the soil had no depth, but when the sun rose and scorched it, it began to wither for lack of roots" (verses 5-6).

The Compromisers. Everyone is born with a political instinct. To one degree or another we recognize the need for compromise if we are to achieve the "art of the possible" (Aristotle). Unfortunately, some people are so captivated by the possibility of compromising that they make it a way of life. Any number of reasons can cause this. Sometimes it is an immature fear of assuming serious responsibility; at other times, a fixation on oneself as the center of the universe.

Compromisers hate the anxiety that comes from tension. They see the tension only in destructive terms and fail to recognize its creative possibilities. The Word of the Cross, with its clear challenge, demands too much responsibility from the compromiser. Beyond this, the sheer attractiveness of worldliness nourishes the compromising instinct to the level of a virulent infection. Caught between the thorns of anxiety in the face of responsibility and a captivation with the movable feast of the world, compromisers eventually give up on religion.

Anyone who plants the evangelical seed in the heart of a compromiser should unhappily await a projected disaffection with the kingdom. Their anxiety and fixation on the passing fancies of this world lead only to nonacceptance.

"What was sown among briers is the man who hears the message, but then worldly anxiety and the lure of money choke it off" (verse 22).

The Truly Open. Although evangelization obviously will have its failures, it also will have joyous successes. In every audience there is a consciousness that is truly open. There are many genuine searchers for truth. Millions of restless hearts have determined to seek until their spirits rest in the kingdom. The Truly Open are not distracted by fads or thrills. They are not put off by anxiety in the face of responsibility. Riches and worldliness do not deter them. They do not suffer Macbeth's tragic "avarice":

There grows in my most ill-compos'd affection
Such a stanchless avarice, that, were I king,
I should cut off the nobles for their lands.

—Macbeth, act 4, scene 3

The Truly Open have never lost the sense of wonder that keeps them turned in to the "more than" of life. They have the wisdom not to reduce reality to a manageable package. Life is too full of mystery and transcendence. Planted in the consciousness of the Truly Open, the evangelical seed finds the good earth. "But what was sown on good soil is the man who hears the message and takes it in. He it is who bears a yield of a hundred — or sixty — or thirty fold" (verse 23).

The Weeds (Mt. 13:24-30)

Christ's second parable about the weeds and the wheat illustrates the realism one must have in evaluating people in the kingdom. All entry into the kingdom is a time of grace and baptismal purity. Being truly open is no guarantee that one is perfect. The wheat field will be plagued by the weeds. Grace abounds, but sin abides to tear the members of the kingdom away from their ideals.

It is this sinfulness of some members of the kingdom that both discourages the faithful ones and drives away those who might otherwise be ready to accept Christ. The weeds have sprouted in every age of the church's history. Purists want those weeds thrown out of the kingdom. They want them uprooted and only a perfect face shown to the world. Christ advises otherwise: "Pull up the weeds and you might take the wheat with them" (verse 29). Regardless of the embarrassment and anxiety the weeds cause, they serve a purpose. They challenge the believers (the wheat) to retain utter confidence in the purity of the kingdom, the power of grace and the final victory of Jesus.

The Mustard Seed and Leaven (Mt. 13:31-33)

These two parables convey the same message. The kingdom begins small and grows slowly. Every gardener is aware of the mystery of growth, just as every parent is. The glorious delight that comes from watching the inner power take shape in leaves and branches, and flowers and fruit, communicating life's mystery. It is the same with the kingdom—so much of its growth is hidden.

Now that many people are beginning to bake their own bread again, the parable of the yeast once more is becoming a relevant image. Watching the little lump of dough imperceptibly expand into a fluffy loaf ready for the oven is at once a simple and profound analogy for appreciating the hidden growth capability of the kingdom. The lesson comes at two levels. Do not try to hurry the growth of the church. Allow for a patient inner grace to perform its miracle of expansion. This does not absolve each believer from evangelical effort. Every believer is a seed and a yeast. But small beginnings combined with an appreciation of slow inner growth (the mystery of grace inter-acting with consciousness) is a better guarantee of a long-lasting oak tree and a fine-textured loaf.

The Pearl (Mt. 13:44-46)

In recent years, the church has been urged to become more relevant to our culture. To reinforce this the image of the Seed has been used. Seeds, after all, are earthy and share the common concerns of the ground. The evangelical message ought to be a response to human need. The problem is in the word "relevance." Relevant to what? To needs, of course. But to what needs? To man's needs for justice, honor, a decent living, respect, and self-realization. Recent discussions have confined relevance mainly to these areas. But man also has other needs, among them the spiritual and religious.

The kingdom is a pearl as well as a seed. Like a pearl, it is a reservoir of divine beauty and radiance that responds to profound spiritual hunger and thirst. It was probably no accident that a renewed interest in the occult has accompanied an increased under-standing of relevance. It is a reminder that people do not live by bread alone. Jesus asks us to keep alive the relevance of the kingdom as both a pearl and a seed: "The kingdom of heaven is like a merchant's search for fine pearls. When he found one really valuable pearl, he went back and put up for sale all that he had and bought it" (verse 46).

The Net (Mt. 13:47-50)

Today's cultural emphasis is on the need for understanding and acceptance. Quite correctly, psychology urges us to withhold judg-ment and to help people live without threat and come to self under-standing. This reflects both compassion and charity. It can, however, be deceptive when it excludes the possibility of moral judgment.

Helping people to see themselves and solve their inner problems should not rob them of facing up to a responsibility that involves judgment about good and evil. Jesus clearly made a judgment about the advocates of antifaith. Now, he reminds us that the kingdom is like a net that brings all kinds of people aboard and that some of them will be thrown overboard. In other words, the day will come when it is time to get rid of the weeds.

Jesus says that angels will do this. It also is truly an act of self-exile. In the final analysis, refusal of the kingdom is a personal matter. Freedom was misused to reject Christ. Talk of judgment is out of style these days, but it remains an enduring image of the kingdom.

This chapter closes with a "prophet without honor" (verse 57) story. No master is a hero to his valet. A prophet seldom is a hero to the home folks.

We have thus far considered here six of the main parables. The remaining four will be discussed as they appear in the gospel text.

Reflection

1. Do I like to hear a story?
2. Jesus told many stories-parables. He also delivered commands and wisdom sayings. Which touch me more?
3. If I only wanted an emotional high from religion, what could I expect?
4. If I seek a religion that approves of compromising standards and values, what good is such a religion?
5. If I am truly open in my Christianity, how will the seed of God's Word affect me?
6. What is my reaction to "weeds" (sinners) in the church? Do I feel the urge to drive them out? Or seek their reconciliation?
7. What do the parables of the seed and heaven tell me about the mystery of life and my religion?
8. Do I expect religion to be relevant to my need for spirituality and eternal life?
9. Why is my religion like a pearl of great price?
10. Jesus said he was a prophet without honor in his own country. Do I think my faith convictions will always make me liked and accepted?

Prayer

Divine Master, I love your stories. I hear them year after year and never tire of them. Your parable of the seed and the various kinds of reception tell my story very well. I am often too anxious to be thrilled by religion, to get an emotional kick. I can even be faddish in my faith. I know I should be open, be the good ground in which your love and forgiveness takes root. Here is the key to my heart. Open me to your affection.

14   Salome and the Bread Miracle

A Dramatization (Mt. 14:1-12)

Baptist: (Roaring from his cell) Herod, will you take your sister-in-law to bed again this night? Stop pretending it is not adultery. Do not soften it with the sweet excuses of extramarital sex. Send her back to your brother Philip where she belongs.

Herod: (In the palace dining room) I wish I could choke his voice. He's still too popular. The people think he is a prophet.

Herodias: He makes you feel guilty, doesn't he?

Herod: I don't think kings and princes should have to put up with public insults and embarrassments. But, you are right, he fills me with shame.

Herodias: Perhaps your conscience is still too tender. You still think like a child and fear the disapproval of John as though he were your parent.

Herod: I'm full of fears. His accusations haunt my dreams. He shouts at me night and day like a madman. The people say he has the madness of God.

Herodias: You take him much too seriously. And you are far too sensitive to the people.

Herod: The Romans favor me because I keep the people quiet.

Herodias: The people are not as devoted to John as you think. He's much more dangerous alive than dead.

Baptist: Get rid of her, Herod. The kingdom of heaven is at hand. A new age is beginning. Repent!

Herodias: Dear Herod, forget that so-called prophet. Cheer up, it is your birthday. The music will drown out his ravings. My daughter Salome will divert you. She has been practicing a new dance for you.

Herod: She is a beautiful girl.

Herodias: Relax and let Salome dance away your fears.
Salome dances.

Herodias: (At conclusion of dance) Are you pleased, my lord?

Herod: She has given me my first ten minutes of peace in months. Salome, you deserve a kingdom. Tell me what you would like. I'll grant you your fondest wish.

Salome: Bring me the head of John the Baptizer on a platter.

Herod: (To himself) Release at last. This enchanting girl convinces me of what I should do. Still, I must not act hastily. Politically, it can be divisive. Demonstrations in the streets. Roman frowns. Worse yet, I have a strange love for John. Deep down, I know he is right and I admire his integrity. I am no child fearing a parent figure in John. I did not push my way to power by being naive. But I am casting my lot with evil. I know what I am doing. And now I am ashamed to go back on my word before all the guests.

Salome: His head, my lord!

Herod: Executioner, do as she wishes.

Baptist: I will not die, Herod. You will hear me in your dreams. I will haunt your conscience. I will live. It is you who will die. Believe in the kingdom, my brother! Believe in. . . .

Bread Miracle (Mt. 14:13-21)

Jesus mourned the martyrdom of his cousin John. He needed to be alone and passed the days of mourning in solitude in a retreat across the lake of Galilee. He pondered that with the death of John the full leadership in the ministry of the kingdom now passed to him. In contemporary political jargon, John had been a perfect advance man. The prophet made way for the messiah, and now that messiah must act.

Ancient prophecy foresaw that in messianic days God would prepare a banquet for the people. Just as God fed Israel with manna in the desert, God would, in messianic times, prepare a table for all members of the kingdom. The bread miracle was a first fulfillment of this promise and a foretaste of the Eucharist that would be the bread of life for all believers.

A massive crowd pursued Jesus to his resting place in the desert.

They did not demonstrate in the streets as Herod had feared, but instead rallied to John's successor in hope of direction and leadership. They sought the shepherd and asked for food. Jesus nourished them not only spiritually but also physically by the wonder of the bread miracle. With five loaves and a couple of fish, he fed five thousand people that day. This miracle was considered so important in apostolic times that it was written up in all four gospels. In John 6 it is followed by the well known Bread of Life dialogue in which Jesus explains the greater wonder of the Eucharistic Sacrament. If baptism signified entrance into the kingdom of heaven, the Supper of the Lord is the sacramental feast for the believers in the kingdom.

This Sacrament is the perennial reminder of life-long commitment to the kingdom. Thrill seekers and compromisers will in the long run go away. Since the evangelical seed finds no real root in them, neither will the Lord's Supper be able to call them to enduring dedication.

Walking on the Water (Mt. 14:22-33)

Prove to me that you're no fool
Walk across my swimming pool
Then I'll let you go free.

—Herod's song in *Jesus Christ Superstar*

The cynical tone of Superstar's song catches the quality of disbelief that many hold toward Jesus' divine sonship as illustrated in the story of the storm at sea. The gospel writers normally tell this story along with that of the bread miracle since both are strong faith narratives.

After the loaves miracle, Jesus wants to be alone. He sends the apostles back across the lake. A storm comes up and the boat founders. The frightened apostles see Christ coming to them, walking on the water. Terrified they think he is a ghost. Jesus assures them, "Get hold of yourselves! It is I. Do not be afraid!" (verse 27). Peter says that if it be the Lord, he should bid him to share in the miracle, permit him to walk on the water, but quickly loses confidence and sinks into the waves. Jesus rescues him with a rebuke about the thinness of his faith. The story ends with an act of adoration, "Beyond doubt you are the Son of God!" (verse 33).

Jesus is the Lord. Only the Lord can be the master of the waters and the storms. It requires radical trust and faith to believe in him. Superstar's Herod said he would believe if Jesus would walk across his swimming pool. But Peter saw an even greater marvel: Jesus striding through a tempest-torn sea. Peter thought he believed but he really didn't. The marvel alone does not produce faith. Thrill-seeking is no answer. The marvel is a sign of a deeper reality of the kingdom. This is what calls for faith.

Herod wanted a religious stunt. Peter was intrigued by the sight of Christ walking on the water. Neither could see what was really going on. Herod, of course, never learned. Peter and the other apostles did. They saw beyond the wonder to the heavenly reality and confessed in faith the Lordship of Christ.

Reflection

1. Do I notice the energy and force of my conscience? Does it help me behave in a Christian manner?
2. How does the Baptist affect the conscience of Herod?
3. What strategy does Herodias use to dull Herod's conscience?
4. Why would a powerful ruler, already married, be so influenced by Salome's dance?
5. The imprisoned Baptist realizes he is in deep trouble. What moved him to put his life in peril by assaulting Herod's conscience?
6. Has my conscience ever moved me to make difficult decisions?
7. All four gospels report the bread miracle. What was so important about it to receive such notice?
8. What aspect of Christ's identity is revealed by his walking on the water?
9. What does Peter's sinking into the sea tell me about my own faith journey?
10. If I saw a miracle would my faith automatically be deepened?

Prayer

My Savior, I thank you for the gift of conscience. There are times when I feel its force and energy moving me to Christian behavior. I must confess that I also have tried to quiet its insistent challenge to goodness. I appreciate St. Paul's words about not doing what I should and doing what I ought not. My soul can be a battlefield between good and evil. You are the Bread of Life who can nourish me in the single-hearted pursuit of goodness. Feed me, Lord.

15   Religious Hypocrisy

The Pharisees (Mt. 15:1-20)

It is a pity that the pharisees have become synonymous with religious hypocrites. They did not start out that way and in Christ's time many of them were sincere, devout people. The pharisees were a group of religious scholars and teachers who came into existence two centuries before Christ. They were the successors of the mystical Hasidism, most of whom were martyred during the Greek conquest.

In a deeply religious society such as Judaism, the pharisees naturally exercised political power. They leaned toward pacifism, but at times did support military causes, especially those that sought freedom from Rome. More importantly, they were religious educators, teachers of the Torah. They maintained that the Torah (one Law, the first five books of the bible) was not only the five books, but also the sacred oral tradition that had survived so many centuries. Because of the pharisees' support of oral tradition, the sayings of the great prophets were added to the canonized Scripture in 200 B.C. and ever-compelling Wisdom sayings were included in 90 B.C.

The pharisees were skilled in adapting biblical writings to new developments in history and culture. Far from being liturgical conservatives, they encouraged new rituals for the Temple and were influential in establishing the festival of Hanukkah, which is celebrated by our Jewish brethren close to the Christian observance of Christmas. In their teachings they developed speculations about angels and the resurrection of the body, which was somewhat ironic since they, in large part, did not recognize the messiah when he came and denied the resurrection of Jesus.

Their emphasis on strict obedience to religious laws must be understood in terms of their efforts to preserve Judaism through two centuries of social and cultural turmoil. Greek and Roman occupations, in combination with attempts by conquerors to dilute, if not destroy, Judaism, prompted the pharisees to insist on strict conformity and discipline when the ranks of the covenant people might be dispersed.

The unhappy fallout from this stress on a strict legal obediences to the Torah was a de-emphasis on God's love for man and the growth of religious hypocrisy. Their zeal for the Torah is reflected in Psalms:

How I love your law O Lord!
It is my meditation all the day.

—Ps. 119:97

Many pharisees were people of integrity and obvious holiness. It was they who sustained the belief that the divine glory (the shekinah) was present in their work and worship. The pharisee Nicodemus, among others, exemplifies this genuine strain of devout pharisees.

He came to Jesus in a desire to grasp the meaning and hope of the kingdom. He was the only one to raise his voice to the religious leaders and ask them for fairness to Christ at his trial and it was he who participated in the burial services for Christ's body.

This background should be kept in mind when we read about Christ's condemnation of religious hypocrisy. The point was not the pharisees' historical greatness, but their present blindness. A good movement had gone sour. Jesus criticized them for ostentatious piety, for tithing wild herbs (Mt. 23:3), for straining their drinking water lest they swallow an impure gnat (Mt. 23:4), and for making large donations to the temple so they would not have the greater financial burden of taking care of their parents (Mt. 15:3-6). Christ's story comparing the humility of the publican with the haughty piety of the pharisee perhaps best dramatizes the substance of the critique of religious hypocrites.

Hypocrisy is a perennial pitfall for the devout. Their dedication to pious deeds often gradually blinds them to the reason for the deeds, namely, to give glory to God, and love and justice to people. They concentrate on means, not ends. They forget the purpose of religion and therefore become fair game for the trap of hypocrisy.

Jesus probably would not have been so severe on the pharisees if they had not been so central to the religious life of the people and, therefore, such major obstacles to the light of the kingdom. In addition, they were not passive observers of his work, but took an aggressive and hostile stand against what he was trying to do. Ultimately, they would back the forces coalescing to destroy him.

The Canaanite Woman (Mt. 15:21-28)

Evangelization always begins with the official community of believers, then spills out to other searchers after truth. This is the lesson of the encounter between Jesus and the Canaanite woman. Wearied by the demands of the ministry, Jesus and the apostles were resting in the region of Tyre and Sidon (present day Lebanon).

What makes the story appealing and compelling is that it emphasizes the diligence of the searcher more than that of the preacher. Successful persistence is always an attractive quality. The Canaanite woman excels in the talent for understanding failure as a motivation for success. She is a memorable example of the importance of ardent pursuit in spiritual matters:

Woman: Lord have pity on me! My daughter is troubled by a demon.

(Jesus ignores her)

Woman: (Shouting all the louder) Lord, didn't you hear me. My daughter is very sick. She is possessed.

Jesus: My mission is only to the lost sheep of the house of Israel.

(This is the evangelical strategy, to call the community of believers to conversion first. It is a reply that seems both to resolve to adhere to the plan for mediating the kingdom's message and healing, and to test the persistence of the woman.)

Woman: (kneeling humbly) Help me, Lord.

Jesus: It is not right to take the food of sons and daughters and throw it to the dogs.

(By most standards this is an unfeeling and harsh answer. By reemphasizing the confining of the message to Israel and using the Hebrew word for pagans — dogs — Jesus seems to be going beyond the call of duty in testing her.)

Woman: Please, Lord, even the dogs eat the leavings that fall from the master's table.

Jesus: Woman, you have great faith! Your wish will come to pass. Your daughter is cured.

(Who could resist the charm and the steadfastness of this believing woman? Jesus declares his admiration for her great faith. She is not deterred by master plans. She has a sick daughter, knows who can help and remains adamant until she is heard. The message is evident.)

Reflection

1. Did I realize that not all pharisees were religious hypocrites?
2. What did pharisees contribute to the development of the Old Testament?
3. Why did the pharisees emphasize obedience to religious laws?
4. Was Jesus condemning all the pharisees of his day when he spoke so damagingly about religious legalism?
5. What should I know and admire about the pharisee Nicodemus?
6. The fourth commandment was originally designed to remind the adult children of aged parents to look after their welfare. What words of Jesus in this chapter reflect that?
7. Daily life bogs me down in its details. I forget the goals. How can I think more of ends and less of means to those ends?
8. The story of the Canaanite woman dramatizes that a "no" is only the beginning of a dialogue. Am I capable of such faith persistence?
9. What first principle of evangelization does Jesus state in his meeting with the Canaanite woman?
10. Am I capable of the humility and charm the Canaanite woman exercised in her relationship with Christ?

Prayer

Compassionate Lord, you could be stern with religious people who use religion to harm people. You also responded with sensitivity and understanding to a mother dedicated to her daughter's cure. I hope that I will never misunderstand the role of my faith, moving me to hurt people. I also pray that I will always have Christian compassion toward others in need. I ask you for this grace.

16 Thou Art Peter

Reprise (Mt. 16:1-12)

The first twelve verses of this chapter repeat previous themes. Once again Jesus is asked for a sign and he replies with the Easter image of Jonah. He reverses the leaven image of the kingdom to apply it to the pharisees. Kingdom leaven indicates the mystery of hidden growth and the quiet influencing of others toward the good. Pharisee leaven points to the hidden growth of evil and the effect of religious hypocrisy of faith.

Peter Chosen as Leader (Mt. 16:13-20)

The scene is Caesarea Philippi, a city built by Prince Philip on the slopes of Mount Hermon. It is named after both Philip, the founder and the Caesar of the Tiberias. Philip purposely located the city near a cave shrine, holy to Greeks and Romans. There they worshipped the god Pan. Since adoration of Pan was associated with nature's fertility, human mating rites were performed as part of the cult. The mouth of the cave called the Gates of Pan, contained a stream that was the main source of the Jordan river.

The setting, then, was one of rock sculpture, conveying a sensual yet mystical mood generated by a primitive nature religion. There is the peculiar awe associated with the primary sources of bodies of water. There is the majesty of leadership imposed by the double name of a powerful prince and a Roman emperor. Christ's selection of Caesarea Philippi, by the Gates of Pan and the source waters of the Jordan, is a symbolic setting almost too good to be true. It is as though a master dramatist freely associated every possible conducive element so that the words and events could proceed with a spontaneity that required no prompting.

Jesus opens with the dialogue.

"Who do people say the Son of Man is?" (verse 13).

The gospel writers note frequently that Jesus uses the term Son of Man as a self-characterization. The expression is weighted with two meanings: (1) humanity and (2) apocalypse. The prophet Ezekiel uses the phrase over seventy times. He employs Son of Man to mean a sinful and weak human being. Jesus uses the Ezekiel meaning to refer to his own humanness—but without the weakness of sin.

Daniel 7:14 also dwells on a Son of Man image. He pictures the Son of Man coming in the clouds of heaven. Scholars speak of this scene as an apocalypse, a revelation. Apocalyptic language occurs in scripture during the times of great turmoil. It uses the idiom of catastrophe, storms and darkened suns, and social upheavals to beckon the appearance of spiritual judgment. Jesus will use just such talk in his own Last Judgment sermon.

It is not always clear whether Christ's listeners think of the Ezekiel meaning (humanity) or the Daniel significance (apocalypse) when they hear Jesus speak of himself as Son of Man. The gospels do not record anyone asking Jesus why he called himself Son of Man, let alone which meaning of the phrase he might have had in mind. Nor do they have anybody else calling him that. Nor does any other New Testament figure apply that description to himself.

In any case, Jesus raises the question about his identity. His apostles have been with him for some time and Jesus wants to know how people view him. The apostles are anything but united in their opinion. They reflect the popular rumors of the time that were associated with reincarnation theories. Obviously, they considered Jesus an extraordinary person. In that, they echo the people's opinion: Jesus is a reincarnation of John the Baptist, Elijah, Jeremiah or some major prophet.

Reincarnation is a persistent belief in many cultures and many religions. For some, such as the Hindus, it is a major tenet. For others, it sometimes surfaces as a sub-belief or part of fashionable avowal of occult phenomena. Judaism, which had not settled on a clear view of immortality, seemed to be especially prone to reincarnation as a possible solution. Of course, we should not separate the superstitious belief in ghosts from these intimations of reincarnation.

Jesus surely knew what people were saying about him. The

apostles' answer simply confirmed it and set the stage for a deeper question: "Who do you say that I am?" (verse 15). There was silence. That silence is not just the result of a fear of giving the wrong answer. Jesus is their friend and leader, and a person of unbelievable wonder and depth. What words could they possibly find to capture his meaning? Who had ever known such a man as this? Is it possible to find words that do justice to a description of Jesus? For eleven of the apostles, the answer is no. He is either beyond words or they are simply too tongue-tied to finds words.

Finally, Peter speaks, "You are the Messiah, the Son of the living God!" (verse 16).

The richness of Peter's reply is dazzling. In the light of God's fire, he speaks as though uttering an oracle. The words form on his lips, not like the easy declarations of logic, let alone the subtle conclusions of inductive reasoning. He is neither a Shakespeare nor a Plato, yet his reply possesses an eloquence and a clarity worthy of both.

What neither the religious learning of the pharisees, the peasant cunning of the people nor the sheer intimacy of apostleship could discern, Peter is the first to see. His words are not the result of cold calculations, ignorant superstition or flattery. He is far too innocent to resort to such tactics.

Peter's words are born in ecstacy. The blunt fisherman has become a spiritual oracle because the Holy Spirit has taken hold of his heart and offered his mind that luminous insight. Given divine inspiration, Peter is privileged to be the first apostle to see, know and declare the real meaning of Jesus.

Jesus replies almost as one overcome with joy, as one hearing the purest echo that can ultimately be sensed. For that brief and shining moment on the slopes of Caesarea Philippi, Peter and the Infinite are as one:

Blest are you, Simon, son of John!
No mere man has revealed this to you, but my heavenly Father.
I, for my part declare to you,
You are Rock, and on this rock I will build my church
And the jaws of death shall not prevail against it.
I will entrust to you the keys of the kingdom of heaven.

—Verses 18-19

With those words Jesus anoints the leader who will carry on his work after he is gone. Could Peter know that those words would one day be carved by Michelangelo at the base of a dome crowning St. Peter's Basilica in the city of Rome? Today, millions of pilgrims can see these words clearly etched in that dome and hear a choir sing them to the music of Palestrina.

Jesus tells Peter that the jaws of death (or, in the old translation, the Gates of Hell) will not prevail against his leadership. He speaks of demonic gates while gazing at the jaws of Pan. Lest anyone be mistaken, he draws attention to the wonder of Peter's confession. It came not from the gossip of the crowd nor through arduous reasoning; not from man but from the divine overshadowing. Peter's words were spoken out of religious ecstacy.

It is clear that this was no idle moment. Christ's previous debates with the pharisees, his rejection at Nazareth, his experience of people clawing at him for miracles without reaching for the kingdom—all these awoke in him the brooding and foreboding of tragedy ahead. Debates and opposition would go beyond academic disagreement. Savage cruelties waited in the shadows, and Jesus was the first to realize.

Reflection

1. Why was the choice of Caesarea Philippi an inspired one for naming Peter as leader?
2. Is it surprising that the Apostles should be confused by Jesus' question about his identity? Should they have known better?
3. What is the difference between the term *Son of Man* as used in Ezekiel and as employed in Daniel?
4. What inspired Peter to speak the real identity of Jesus?
5. If I am asked to say who Jesus is, what do I say?
6. Where does my identification of Jesus come from?
7. Peter is mentioned 195 times in the New Testament as compared to 130 times for all the rest of the Apostles. How might this fact relate to Christ's choice of Peter as leader?
8. Jesus changed Simon's name to Peter (Rock). What is the importance of such a name change?

9. In choosing names for my children, do I not have a special purpose in mind?
10. The jaws of hell will not overcome the church. What examples of this could I name from the church's experience?

Prayer

Lord of history, you provided Peter as a leader for your church. You knew that a church must be an organization as well as a community. Someone must be in charge after you are gone. Peter was not ready at Caesarea Philippi, but after his denial and repentance and his anointing by the Spirit, he realized his calling. I am grateful for your providence. I pray for the successors of St. Peter, the popes, that they will be strengthened in their demanding role.

17 The Transfiguration

Glory on the Mountain (Mt. 17:1-8)

Among any group of people some inevitably are more special
than others. Jesus singles out Peter, James and John from the apostles
as unique witnesses of his transfiguration on the mountain and his
agony in the garden. Peter, the leader, John the beloved apostle and
James, who would become the first apostle to die for Christ, are the
three chosen to receive a foretaste of Christ's death and resurrection.

Matthew does not name the mountain. Tradition calls it Thabor,
probably because that is the most majestic mountain in Palestine. It
overlooks the plains of Esdraelon where Deborah, a Joan of Arc of
the Old Testament, led the Israelites to a victory against a powerful
Bronze Age enemy. The village of Naim is located on those plains.
Jesus raised to life the body of a teenage boy, the son of a widow
from that village. Those plains apparently still have some future history to live out. On them the battle of Armageddon (another name for
the plains of Esdraelon, actually its west sector) will take place. "The
devils then assembled the kings in a place called in Hebrew
'Armageddon' " (Rv. 16:16). This war on the west corner of
Esdraelon is supposed to be the final battle of mankind. After it
comes the end of the world and the Second Coming of Christ.

Quite likely it is on top of the mountain overlooking this plain
that Jesus appeared to the favored three in all his heavenly glory. Six
days before, Peter had received his first divine shock, his initial
religious experience of the Father. It led him to confess Jesus as Messiah and Son of God. Now, Peter is again washed in God's fire. This
time however, James and John also are initiated into the brotherhood
of infinite revelation.

Jesus, the light of the world, becomes pure light for the apostles.
Moses and Elijah appear and talk with him. The Lawgiver Moses

and the one who restored the Law, Elijah, speak to the one who has come to fulfill the whole meaning of the Law. The old covenant, its origins and its reformation converse with the new covenant of fulfillment.

Peter, who is now conscious of his leadership role, cries out that he will build three tents for the awesome guests. He is already becoming the organizer and institutionalizer. His reference to tent-building leads some to think that the story reflects the Jewish Feast of Tents, a religious festival connected with the harvest, a celebration as popular among Jews as Christmas is among Christians today.

Basically, the Feast of Tents was the Jewish Thanksgiving Day, with much dancing, eating and thanking of God for a joyful harvest. The expression "tents" refers to the temporary tents made of branches under which the people slept during the harvest days in the fields.

After Peter spoke, a cloud rested over them and from it came the voice of God telling them that Jesus was God's Son. This cloud was clearly the same as the pillar of cloud that led Israel through the desert and like the cloud that rested on the ark of the covenant showing God's presence and unity with the people. Hebrews called it the *Shekinah*, which means "the glory," the divine presence.

On the mount of the Transfiguration the two themes of Matthew's Gospel come together: the kingdom and the glory. The invisible kingdom for a small moment reveals itself as the manifestation of God's glory. The scene was so awesome that the apostles fell to the ground and hid their eyes in fear. No one can look upon the face of God and live.

In other words, the blinding truth of God is too great for earthly assimilation all at once. It is enough that the light has been given and the corresponding assurance has been communicated. Truth both reveals and conceals itself. It reveals in that it reminds us of the meaning it has to communicate. It conceals because it has more to pass on and asks us to keep up the search. This is why we can keep meditating on old truths and continue to find more in them as the years pass.

The vision ended with Jesus raising them up and assuring them they had no need to be afraid. Some commentators have noted the similarity between this vision and the experience of the agony in the Garden. In both cases the visible aspect of Jesus is radically changed. Here, the dominant color is the white light of glory. At Gethsemane it is the red blood of agony.

On both occasions the same three witnesses are present, and Jesus is spoken to by the Father. On Thabor the apostles are buried in the sleep of awe. At Gethsemane they slumber in the daze of post-banquet fatigue. Prophets speak to the Lord of Thabor. Angels comfort the Lord of the Garden. The mood of covenant pervades these two events. Thabor speaks of the new covenant's glorious fulfillment in the kingdom and the glory. Gethsemane announces the price of the new covenant which must be written in suffering and blood.

The two stories are Easter and Good Friday in reverse. As the tradition of the church points out, Jesus wanted the favored three to see the glory as a comfort and trust factor when they face the overwhelming disappointment of the suffering that is to come. For that reason it is important to link the prophecy of the passion (verses 22-23) with this scene. Jesus cools their ecstasy with a prediction of his future humiliation. According to Matthew, this fills them with grief. Mark is far more realistic. He says that Peter both opposes the idea and refuses to acknowledge that it will happen. He appears to demand that Jesus must see that it does not occur.

Jesus replies with a ferocity typical of his approach to any attempt to divert him from the duties of the kingdom. "Get out of my sight, you Satan. You are not judging by God's standards, but by man's!" (Mark 8:33). It is a fierce rebuke, but it does show how much is at stake in establishing the kingdom. From now on the aspect of the cross looms ever more prominent in Matthew's story.

Elijah/Possession/Temple Tax (Mt. 17:9-27)

The remaining thoughts in this chapter take up the legend that Elijah must come before the kingdom is founded. The second coming of Elijah was a popular belief based upon the concept that he still needs to die. He was privileged to visit God in a fiery chariot but he must come back and go through the human destiny. It will not be too disappointing for him because he will soon share in the destiny of the glory of messianic times. It will be a joy to those who observe it because it signals the fulfillment of their hopes. Jesus solves their problem by saying that the second coming of Elijah occurred symbolically in the life of the Baptist. Jesus is the messiah whom the Elijah/Baptist heralded.

Christ's exorcism of the possessed boy is another item of evangelization in body talk. Here the emphasis is on the faith of the one who works miracles.

The paying of the Temple Tax exemplifies that Jesus both obeys the Law and gives it further meaning.

The next chapter contains the final details before Christ begins his paschal journey to Jerusalem.

Reflection

1. In my life, who are the people more special to me than anyone else? Does this help explain Christ's choice of Peter, James and John to be with him at the Transfiguration?
2. Mount Tabor is the traditional site of the Transfiguration. It overlooks the plains of Esdraelon. What biblical stories are associated with Esdraelon?
3. Some scholars compare Tabor with Gethsemane. What is the same and what is different in the two events?
4. Why did Peter speak of constructing tents?
5. The cloud is an image that often appears in Scripture. What do these biblical clouds remind me of?
6. How does the Transfiguration bring together Christ's teaching about the kingdom and the revelation of the divine glory?
7. When I have a deep and pleasant religious feeling, how would I react when reminded of the Cross that goes with my faith?
8. Why is Jesus so severe in calling Peter a "Satan?"
9. Do I know of exorcisms happening today?
10. What does Christ's paying of the Temple tax reveal about his attitude to law?

Prayer

Transfigured Lord, I join Peter, James and John in adoring your glory. In my daily life I forget the attitudes of awe and reverence. I should know that when I reverence your glorious presence I will also reverence myself and the mystery of others. I am grateful for the gift of reverence. May your glory ever stand before my spirit.

18 Lost Sheep and Merciless Officials

Born Again (Mt. 18:1-5)

The apostles ask Jesus, "Who is of greatest importance in the kingdom of heaven?" (verse 1). Like a master teacher, Jesus illustrated his reply. He calls a little child over and places him in the middle of their circle. If they change and become like this child, they will enter the kingdom, be born again. Adulthood demands managing the complexity of life. The problem is, the complexity tends to drown us in a morass of details. After a while the adult accepts the confusion and the breathless race as a way of life. He fails to push on to the depths of simplicity: organized innocence.

Jesus clearly wants people who rise above details, information overload and rapid social change to a universal vision that ties everything together. The kingdom provides this, and members who enter it must be prepared to acquire the universal horizon against which the millions of bits of information and movement can be seen as a pattern of meaning giving glory to God.

We can never be children again; we can never return to the nursery. But we can go forward to the second naivete, the new childlike universality that brings it all together. That is what makes little children so charming. They remind us of a goal ahead. It is what makes great people great: they are simple, yet profound. They have not forgotten complexity, but have woven it together into a pattern imbued with divine colors and significance.

Scandal (Mt. 18:6-9)

Jesus delivers a sharp admonition against those who would

deliberately give scandal: A "couldn't-care-less" attitude is the opposite of the ideal of passionate caring that all members of the kingdom should espouse. World weariness (what the Germans call *weltschmerz*) produces the cynicism that leads to the basic scandal of convincing others that there is no kingdom, that meaning is a senseless ideal and faith, a foolish project. When smart people take it upon themselves to humiliate and mislead searchers for truth, they give scandal. They close off the search and give the impression that we are all trapped in a room of raving madmen from which there is no exit. Jesus prescribes a savage cure: cut off the hand, amputate the foot, gouge out the eye that is the cause of such ravings. While this is not to be taken literally, Jesus is serious on the matter of purging the self of the cynical behavior that leads to scandal.

Lost Sheep (Mt. 18:10-14)

A good shepherd leaves the ninety-nine sheep to look for the one that is lost. A good leader takes time from the saved to search out the ones who are missing. A lazy leader spends all the time saving the saved. It is easier that way. Excuses abound: "It takes all my time just to minister to my congregation. Parish activities swallow up all my energies. I have no time for all those lost ones."

Christ says the measure of a great leader is that he or she assumes the saved will be mature enough to take care of themselves. It is the sick who need a physician. Precisely because the saved *are* saved, they are cooperating with inner grace and can free the leader for fresh evangelical work. Healthy congregations do not need incessant coddling from their leaders. Presumably, what makes them healthy is that they can stand on their own. Religious leaders must make the ninety-nine aware of this so that they will not raise an outcry when they devote their energy to the lost ones.

Millions are already in the kingdom. But literally billions are not. True, they may have a consciousness of God, but they have not heard the fullness of the Gospel. They should be given a chance.

Fraternal Correction (Mt. 18:15-18)

One of the most universal signs of human frailty is the persistent habit of discussing another's faults with everyone except the person in question. Talking behind other people's backs is as widespread as crabgrass. It is one of the major reasons why the love that should bind the people of the kingdom together is so often diluted.

Today's group therapy and confrontation sessions basically adopt what Jesus called for so long ago. Has someone wronged you? Go and tell him about it, not someone else. If individual therapy does not work, have a group encounter session. Psychological techniques do not proceed to Christ's next step: "If he ignores them (the encounter group), refer it to the church. If he ignores even the church, then treat him as you would a gentile or tax collector" (verse 17).

These steps obviously do not happen in quick order like the executing of a check list. Faults are acquired over a long period of time. At least equal time must be given to their curing. One should presume good will and expect lapses. The final solution is official removal from the kingdom. This should be rare. (Remember the weeds story?) It usually will occur when the person has fundamentally already self-exiled his presence from the life of the group.

The Power of United Prayer (Mt. 18:19-20)

Shared prayer, group prayer, the need to pray together about a cause, is now on the increase after many years of people praying alone. Jesus urges and praises this kind of praying. It does not exclude solitary prayer, but it is an immensely satisfying and effective form. The testimony from prayer groups is overwhelmingly positive. Such prayer quietly changes the ones praying and reinforces the community aspect of the kingdom of believers.

where two or three are gathered in my name

The Merciless Official (Mt. 18:21-35)

If Cain is avenged sevenfold, then Lamech seventy- sevenfold.
—Gn. 4:24

110

Peter: "When my brother wrongs me, how often must I forgive him? Seven times?"

Jesus: "No, not seven times. I say seventy times seven."

The opening quotation from Genesis provides the background for Peter's question. It refers to the savage law of reprisal and revenge that passed as moral behavior in a cruel age. Lest we become too prim in judging those "bad old days," we might reflect on the presence of similar behavior today.

This supposedly enlightened century has witnessed death camps, bombings and killings that would make Cain and Lamech feel right at home. The popularity of violence in films and novels — often direct repetitions of the Cain-Lamech eye-for-eye approach — along with the all too real stories of drug-related crime testify to the thin ice of civilization on which we rest.

How often should the millions who have been wronged forgive? Jesus reverses the law of Cain and Lamech and declares that forgiveness, not revenge, should occur seventy times seven. Jesus, who reflects the love that pours from the kingdom, teaches that massive forgiveness, healing the wrong even before an apology is received, will do much more to reduce the sinfulness of people than will the perpetuation of reciprocal brutalities.

The story of the merciless official who was forgiven a large debt by his creditor but who brutalized those who owed him small debts and thus received a deserved punishment is an illustration of the need for daily forgiveness. As the Our Father puts it: "Forgive us our trespasses, as we forgive those. . ." (Mt. 6:12).

Reflection

1. I hear a lot about being born again today. What do I think it means? What did Jesus mean by it?
2. I know it is a terrible thing to scandalize a child, or anyone for that matter. What examples of scandal do I know?
3. Do I ever feel cynical about life and religion? How do I overcome that?
4. How seriously — or literally — should I take Jesus' words about amputations of limbs? What does he really mean?

5. Would I resent my pastor taking more time to go after lost sheep than looking after my needs?
6. Who occupies most of my energies? Those who need me or those who do not?
7. Do I find it easier to talk about others' faults behind their backs, rather than confronting them?
8. How would I apply Christ's advice about the correction of others?
9. Do I prefer to pray alone or with a group? What do I see as the advantages of each approach?
10. Am I able to forgive others over and over again? Do I have trouble forgiving myself, even when I have received God's forgiveness?

Prayer

Forgiving Lord, your counsel about forgiveness and correction of others is a liberating ideal. I know I would be happier by listening to your advice. You give me the vision of the kingdom. I get stuck in this world's way of doing things. I have joyfully known your forgiveness. I pray that now I will forgive others as you have absolved me.

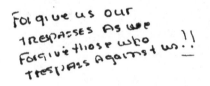

Forgive us our Trespasses As we Forgive those who Trespass Against us!!

Our Father

How many times is too many?

19 The Divorced and the Rich

Divorce (Mt. 19:1-12)

The discussion about divorce in Matthew 19 must be united to the clause about divorce in Matthew 5 and the Old Testament view in Deuteronomy and the Pauline Privilege. In Deuteronomy, Moses allows a husband to divorce his wife if she has been indecent, which most probably refers to an adulterous relationship with another man.

In the Sermon on the Mount (Mt. 5:32) and, in this chapter, verse 9, Jesus repeats the Mosaic law against the contemporary practice of stretching the excuse of the wife's indecency to include anything the husband finds troublesome. He condemns such superficial reasons for divorce.

In chapter 19 Jesus stands opposed to divorce altogether. The ideal was born at the creation of man and woman who are destined to lifelong unity. Moses made an exception, but from the beginning it was not so. The ideal was absolute, monogamous union. It is this original ideal that Jesus is reaffirming.

In New Testament times, St. Paul made an exception to this ideal. Two unbelievers marry. One is converted to the kingdom. The believer is bound to the marriage. If, however, the unbeliever decides to seek a divorce, the believing partner is free to marry again. "God has called you to live in peace" (I Cor. 7:15). Little more is said by Paul, but the usual interpretation is that the right of the believer to fidelity to the kingdom supersedes the original marriage bond if it should or must be broken.

Religious practice has generally followed Christ's injunction against divorce. Exceptions have occurred in the case of annulments and the Pauline Privilege. Some Christian sects have adopted the Mosaic exception of indecency, allowing the innocent partner (man or woman) to divorce and remarry, and continue to receive Communion.

In a time when divorces are so numerous, a second look should be taken at Christ's ideal of enduring monogamy. In addition, compassionate understanding and some deeper thinking should be given to the divorce brethren.

It is not only the playboy culture of the present age that trivializes the monogamous ideal and supports divorce for almost any cause. Cultural practice of Christ's time seemed to be equally lax: "If that (i.e., ideal monogamy) is the case between a man and a woman, it is better not to marry" (verse 10). In other words, if it is necessary to remain monogamous, everyone might just as well remain celibate. Jesus, who chose celibacy as a personal ideal, is quick to note that it must be seen as a grace and a gift. Not everyone can be celibate, only those to whom the grace has been given.

Some are celibate because of a birth disorder. Others have been made celibate, as in the case of the castrated eunuchs used as guards for Mideastern harems. Then there are those who have freely renounced sex for the sake of the kingdom.

Rich People (Mt. 19:16-30)

A rich man asks Jesus how to achieve everlasting life. Christ's reply is in terms of keeping the commandments and the law of love. The rich man happily replies that he has done all of this. Then, says Jesus, "If you seek perfection, go, sell your possessions, and give to the poor" (verse 21).

In this dialogue Jesus is concerned with two points. The first is the difference between a basic practical commitment to the kingdom and the absolute dedication to its ideal. All candidates must subscribe to the former. Only a few can devote themselves completely to incarnating the ideal. For centuries the religious orders have promoted the ideal in terms of the counsel to perfection.

His second point is that the rich will have a more difficult time espousing the counsel to perfection because their wealth is too great to unload. It has been done, of course. Francis of Assisi and many middle class and wealthy people have given up all to follow Christ. But the percentage is probably very small, for it is simpler to go through the eye of the needle than to give up all possessions for the sake of an ideal.

The eye of the needle was apparently a reference to a small gate that camels had great difficulty passing through. Whatever the case, it is self-evident that possessiveness, whether of great wealth or of small amounts, is a lasting human trait. The security it implies and the tenuousness of living militate against any quick decisions about taking on evangelical poverty.

The apostles wonder if anyone could really do it. Jesus says that they can, with the grace of God: "For man, it is impossible, but for God all things are possible" (verse 26). The history of the Christian religion has enough examples to back up this teaching of Jesus. Rich and poor alike have taken up the ideal of evangelical poverty. The percentage may be small in absolute numbers, but it happens often enough for all to realize that it is achievable.

Reflection

1. Am I worried about America's rising divorce rate? What do I think causes such a tragic surge?
2. When Jesus argues absolutely against divorce, he says it was not God's will "in the beginning?" What does he refer to?
3. What is the Pauline Privilege? Why did Paul make this exception?
4. How can the church and society help couples stay faithful to a monogamous union?
5. Do I appreciate that religiously motivated celibacy is a gift of God for the sake of advancing Christ's kingdom?
6. How can celibates and married people strengthen each others' vocations?
7. Do I know rich people to whom Jesus would give his message about their having a harder time living Christian teachings?
8. Do I know rich people who outperform me in their Christian commitment?
9. Was Jesus talking about a needle for sewing?
10. Do Christian ideals discourage me or inspire me?

Prayer

Teacher of wisdom, I experience today divorce among those close to me. I read about greed and the rich. I hear that many challenge celibacy. I am amazed your words about human problems sound as pertinent now as ever. I am saddened that so many, including me, have yet to catch the fire of your insight. I know that a virtuous life demands hard work and grace. You have offered the grace. I must accept it and work harder.

20 The Grape Pickers

Parable (Mt. 20:1-16)

The parable of the grape pickers would hardly be used to support fair labor practices. Obviously it is not intended to do so. What it does illustrate is a dilemma that perennially faces honest, hard-working Christians, namely, the ever-present divine forgiveness that invites the sinner to repentance. It is another version of the story of the prodigal son and the good thief.

Human justice, which possesses such limited horizons, pales even more in the face of divine compassion. The hard-working grape pickers share a common puzzlement with the elder brother in the story of the prodigal son. Why pay the same wages to someone who worked so little? Why give a banquet to one who is so unworthy?

Why? Because the rules in the game of divine grace are not the same as human rules. The divine capacity for forgiveness outdistances any human potential. God loves outrageously and asks us to do the same. Jesus once spoke of bad scandal. In a sense, he is speaking of good scandal in this parable. God scandalizes the just, the good and the worthy. God flaunts love and dares the followers to be as generous. It is a difficult lesson, but it is part of the kingdom package.

It should not be read as an attack on accountability. Enough evidence has been presented to support responsible moral behavior. The lesson of this parable is a logical outgrowth of that of the lost sheep. Jesus focuses our attention on the sheer delight that ought to accompany a conversion. The hard-working grape pickers and the diligent elder brother already enjoy the wealth of the kingdom. They are spiritually rich. Why be small-minded and begrudge the affection lavished on the lost sheep?

No one is forgetting the fidelity of the saved. God is simply giving a party for a newcomer to their company. In essence, Jesus is reminding his loyal comrades that they have a big treasure in heaven and can afford to give much because they have received much. He cautions them not to make morality a mere contract, but to make their hearts as big as their achievement.

This parable and similar stories are not an excuse for ignoring the demands of social justice. The principles of enlightened social concern are sufficiently clear and have been explained. Social concern is not at issue here. What is, is the mysterious vastness of God's continuous forgiving love.

Did This in Them Seem Ambition? (Mt. 20:20-28)

Ambition is a funny thing. It is necessary to goal-seeking, but also can corrupt the seekers. It can make people ruthless. It is to power what avarice is to wealth. Machiavelli says that ambition "is so powerful a passion in the human breast, that however high we reach we are never satisfied."[*] Jonathan Swift claimed that ambition "often puts men upon doing the meanest offices. Thus climbing is performed in the same posture as creeping."[**]

James and John, two of the favored three, come with their mother to ask for the highest places in the kingdom. Jesus immediately nips any first growths of corrupt ambition they may be developing. "Can you drink the cup I am to drink of?" (verse 22). They say they can. Jesus agrees. Like parents offering their young children a realistic view of the future, Jesus advises them they will have much to suffer. Nothing great is ever achieved without enthusiasm—nor without pain.

Jesus tells them to forget ambition and to spurn the worldly ideal of power. Honors will come in the kingdom to those who are worthy. They should forget about the honors and do the job.

Inevitably, the other apostles hear of the episode. Understandably, they become annoyed. In their petulance they demonstrate

---

[*] John P. Bradley, comp. *International Dictionary of Thoughts* [Chicago: Ferguson Publishing Co., 1969], p. 113).
[**] *Ibid.*

that they are equally prone to the temptation of ambition succumbed to by James and John. Jesus gives them all a lecture about power and authority. Kingdom authority should not imitate the authoritarian style of the world. Their job is not to rule but to serve. If they have an ambition to be first, to be ahead of everyone, then they must serve all equally. This image has acquired a special freshness today in the teaching about the servant church. Authority in the church ought to shed any trappings or behavior that would make it seem that it haughtily dominates the souls of people. The purpose of authority in the church is the service of the world. Perhaps everyone in authority in the kingdom should keep a holy card with a picture of the washing of the feet along with this text of Matthew: "Such is the case of the Son of Man who has come, not to be served by others, but to serve" (verse 28).

Jericho's Blind Men (Mt. 20:29-34)

The cure of the two blind men from Jericho seems to be a repetition of the healing story told in Matthew 9:27-31. It is also a second case of the petitioners being scolded for yelling out their prayers for healing. In the story of the Canaanite woman's insistent plea for a cure for her daughter, the apostles tried to stifle her cries which seemed an embarrassment and intrusion to them. On the streets of Jericho, the adoring crowd attempts to squelch the cries of two helpless men. It is not simply that they think the behavior is in bad taste or that it disturbs their superficial religious feelings. They probably had little belief in healing in the first place, and they retained a superstitious morality which regarded blindness as a divine curse for some presumed sins. Worse yet, the men were probably beggars and dirty, obviously not right for the religious set piece they wished to conjure.

Jesus is accustomed to these semi-heartless interferences in his work (Mt. 20:30-34).

"What do you want me to do for you?" he asks.

"Open our eyes!"

He walks over and touches their eyes and they can see immediately. They become his followers.

Reflection

1. How would I explain the grape pickers' story to a grape harvester's labor union?
2. How do I feel when others in my family get better treatment than I do, even though I have been a stronger family member?
3. Is the parable of the grape pickers an excuse for ignoring social justice?
4. If people in my workplace received the same bonus I did, but for half the work I did, how would I react?
5. My ambition gives me energy to perform well. Does it also nourish a killer instinct in me?
6. Do I sympathize with the ambitious James and John? Can I identify with their mother's pushy ways?
7. Is it wrong to desire a position that has authority? When would it be right? What cautions would I offer?
8. What is the purpose of authority in the church and society?
9. If a homeless person yelled at me on a street corner for money, or for not having given enough, how would I feel? Is this the kind of embarrassment the Apostles felt when the blind man of Jericho yelled for a cure?
10. Do I insist that my beggars be polite?

Prayer

Just Savior, I may be more successful with little acts of kindness than doing my bit for justice in the world. I also think my ambition sometimes exceeds my talent. I enjoy giving people orders. I would like to think I'm fair, but I believe I must have a greater commitment to justice. I should not be so bossy. Show me the way through this moral minefield.

21 Holy Week Begins

Palm Sunday (Mt. 21:1-11)

Jerusalem is built on a hill called Zion. Across from the city is the Mount of Olives. Behind the Mount is a village named Bethany. Christ's closest family friends, Martha, Mary and Lazarus, lived there. It was from this suburban and peaceful town that Jesus began his final march to Jerusalem, a five-mile journey.

That journey is re-enacted every Palm Sunday. It begins at Bethany with a public reading of the gospel in which Christ is hailed as the King of Israel taking possession of his capital city, Jerusalem, symbol of the heavenly city. Thousands of pilgrims from all over the world, carrying six-foot olive branches and singing their national hymns, accompany the bishop of Jerusalem in the procession of the palms. They parade down the Mount of Olives, past the Garden of Gethsemane, across the vale of Kedron and enter the Holy City through St. Stephen's Gate. They proceed to the church of St. Anne, mother of the Virgin Mary. It is the traditional site of the home of Anne and her husband Joachim. The ceremonial procession closes with Benediction of the Blessed Sacrament. As the Sacrament is raised, the pilgrims raise and wave their palm branches and cry out:

Hosanna to the Son of David!
Blessed is he who comes in the name of the Lord!
Hosanna in the highest!

—Mt. 21:9

The scene is reminiscent of a medieval mystery play, an act of dramatic worship that captures the spirit of the gospel story of the messianic entry into Jerusalem. The prophet Zechariah had foreseen this messianic joy. "Tell the daughter of Zion, your king comes to you without display, astride an ass, astride a colt, the foal of a beast of burden" (verse 5). Jesus takes possession of the Holy City not in the manner of an imperial general, arrogantly ensconced in a chariot, but in a way resembling a humble servant and heir of the prophets and wise men of Israel.

Palm Sunday has always generated great spiritual joy. In many cultures it has been observed as a reconciliation day. Neighbors, bearing the palms, visit those with whom they have been at odds and ask forgiveness in the Lord. Handel's *Messiah* includes words of the prophet Zephaniah that capture the Palm Sunday mood:

> *Shout for joy, O daughter Zion!*
>   *Sing joyfully, O Israel!*
> *Be glad and exult with all your heart,*
> *The King of Israel, the Lord, is in your midst.*
> *He will rejoice over you with gladness,*
>   *And renew you in his love.*

—Zep. 3:14-17

With Palm Sunday, Matthew begins his account of the Passion and Resurrection of the Lord. The narrative that opens with the palms and ends with Easter is the heart of the Gospel. The first preaching of all the apostles and evangelists was about the death and Resurrection of Jesus. The call to conversion and new life proceeded from it. In fact, the Passion/Resurrection narrative is such a major part of Mark's Gospel that some commentators have called that gospel a "Passion account with a preface."

Matthew's narrative is rich and has been made all the more memorable by Johann Sebastian Bach's *St. Matthew Passion*. The acclamation of Christ as Lord of the heavenly city is a public sign of the rooting of the kingdom for which Jesus has worked for so long. The hosannas that rang out welled up from a mankind hungering for the divine and overcome with joy that their radical reaching is about to be satisfied.

Temple Cleansing (Mt. 21:12-27)

Jesus entered Jerusalem as a messianic King. He proceeds to cleanse the temple as a messianic prophet. If kings are for ruling, prophets are for teaching the real meaning of past tradition, for creating hope in the future and purifying the institutional church when it needs it. Malachi foresaw the special cleansing which Jesus undertakes:

And suddenly there will come to the Temple,
. . . the messenger of the covenant, whom you desire,
Yes, he is coming.
But who will endureth the day of his coming?
For he is like the refiner's fire.
He will purify the sons of Levi.

—Mal. 3:1-5

Prophets comfort the afflicted and afflict the comfortable. Jesus assumes the latter role in purifying the institutional religion from its love affair with commerce and self-serving interests. Servant religion used the institution for the glory of God and the spiritual growth of the people, for a spiritual maturity that includes the whole well-being of the community. Self-serving religion forgets the spiritual needs of the people and uses its power unwisely to aid its own advancement. In servant religion the Temple is a house of prayer. In self-serving religion it is a countinghouse to line the pockets of religious functionaries, to lull the rich and legalistic into paying for salvation and to intimidate the poor with unfounded guilt.

The history of Christianity has seen numerous temple cleansings. The French have an expression, *moyens riches—pauvres d'espirit*, meaning, rich in money, lacking in prayerful spirit. The prophets who act as cleansers are never popular with the institutional leaders, though they usually gain a following from the people, called in Hebrew the *anawim*, the humble and honest people.

It was that way with Jesus the day he cleansed the temple. Children ran through its purified corridors and spiritually awakened pavements, shouting, "Hosanna to the Son of David!" (verse 15). This infuriated the institutional leaders who were the agents of self-serving religion. In striking at their budgets, Jesus was getting too close to home. They could tolerate his abstract sermons about some kingdom and put up with the small waves he made with his cures. They were even amused by the procession of the palms. None of those things threatened them. Now, however, he was exposing their spiritual corruption, touching them where it hurt most—their pocketbooks. By doing so, Jesus revealed what he had been unable to until this point, their empty souls and self-indulgent abuse of religion. What his pointed sermons failed to do, his rage uncovered as he drove their religious-sponsored commercial ventures from the house of God.

Shaken, but resolved not to let Christ get away with it, the leaders demanded to know by whose authority he dared to interfere with temple enterprise. It was a beautiful opening for Jesus and he proposed a question to them: Was the baptism of John of divine origin or merely a human ceremony? If they believed it was divine, they would have to explain their refusal to accept it. If they stated it was simply human, they would anger a majority of the people who treated John as a religious cult figure.

"We don't know," they said lamely.

That being the case, Jesus refused to tell them by what authority he had cleansed the temple. Let them stew in their anger. They would, in fact, do more than stew, for it was the Temple cleansing more than anything else that served as the straw that broke their patience. Plans to kill Jesus developed with great alacrity.

Two Sons (Mt. 21:28-32)

Christ's story of the two sons dramatizes the classic difference between lip service and performance. One son said he would obey his father but did not. The second who refused to obey his father later regretted the refusal and did what he was told. Who was the greater man? Who was really obedient? The apostles agreed it was the second son. Jesus then applied the story to the pious who utter all the correct religious platitudes but do their own thing. Sinners, like whores and tax collectors—the ones who said no—will more likely find the kingdom and ultimately obey the Father's will.

The Vineyard (Mt. 21:33-46)

Virtually all of Jesus' sayings during Holy Week are clear judgments on those who refuse the kingdom and clear accusations concerning their concealed intentions to destroy him. The vineyard is the covenant people. God is the owner. He expects covenant love and fidelity—his share of the grapes. He sends prophets to awaken the people to their religious and moral responsibilities. The tenants kill the holy messengers.

He sends prophets a second time with the same result.

Then he sends his Son. Surely they will not harm him.

But they seized the Son of God, beat him, dragged him outside the vineyard (Holy City) and killed him. The story suggests a scenario predicting the Passion that will occur within a few days. The Lord does not leave it at that. He tells them that the murderers will be driven out of the vineyard and that the kingdom will be given to another.

The tone of Christ's farewell sermons grows more uncompromising as the opposition deepens its hostility and resolve. Good and evil are ready to do battle. The holy martyr to be does not blink.

Reflection

1. Commentators note the fickleness of crowds that cheer Jesus on Palm Sunday and jeer him on Good Friday. Is it possible I would have been capable of such mood swings?
2. What do I do with blessed palm received on Palm Sunday?
3. Prophets comfort the afflicted and afflict the comfortable. How do I react to a prophet afflicting my comfortable ways?
4. Do I believe anger is good? Or is it bad? What about the anger of Jesus in cleansing the Temple?
5. What is the difference between servant religion and self serving religion?
6. Which bothered the religious leaders more, Christ assailing their budgets or their religious legalism?
7. Jesus knew that his cleansing of the Temple would lead to fatal opposition from the religious leaders. Would he not have been wiser to refrain from such confrontation?
8. Which kind of person am I? One who says no, but does what is asked? Or one who says yes and does not do what is asked?
9. Prophets are often persecuted and killed. Who are some modern prophets who suffered and died for their ministry?
10. How would I become more courageous in my convictions?

Prayer

Lord of the Holy City, you took possession of Jerusalem on Palm Sunday. Then you cleansed the temple and so aroused the anger and hostility which led to your death. I have seen your gentleness, meekness and humility. Here I see your power and bravery. May I learn from your example how to blend these differing values. May I have your grace to make it so.

22 Weddings, Taxes and Sadducees

The King Gives a Wedding Feast (Mt. 22:1-14)

Today's divorce rate shows that marriage is in trouble, but weddings are not. A wedding ceremony and its subsequent celebration continues to be among the happiest of human events. Biblical people were no less dedicated to having a good time at a wedding than modern people are. Their marriage customs began with the tent and led to the table and the dance area. Earliest records state that the veiled, bejeweled bride was led to the tent of the groom.

That ritual was modified to performing the marriage under a canopy. Tradition-minded Jews still love to conduct the wedding outdoors under such a tent. If the canopy is not fixed to the ground, it is held by four unmarried young men. The two mothers lead the bride there as the two fathers bring forward the groom. All the features of a good party follow the wedding rite, with feasting, singing, dancing, storytelling and even the use of riddles, as in the story of Samson (Jgs. 14:10-20). As always, there is concern for a good supply of food and drink. The Cana story is an instance of where the wine supply ran out. Jesus was asked by his mother to solve the problem.

In a time when paper was practically nonexistent, messages usually were sent by personal courier. Anyone invited to a wedding was expected to come. Refusal amounted to an insult. In this wedding story recorded by Matthew, the case is much worse. Not only do the invited guests insultingly reject the request, they abuse and even kill the messengers. The king then sends an army to destroy the murderers and burn their property and turns to the poor, the blind and the lame and brings them to his son's marriage feast. Just as today, people are expected to dress up for the important occasion. While it may occasionally be chic to arrive in blue jeans, more formal attire is the acceptable dress, and one can always borrow something for the occasion.

In biblical times, the grooms sometimes provided textiles to the guests so that they could make their own suits and gowns for the wedding. It is easy enough to appreciate how offensive it would be for a guest to arrive not wearing formal clothes. It obviously would be much more so when he had been provided with new material for a proper garment. It is not unknown today to ask an offending or offensive guest to leave a party. It would have been even more expected in the case of this harassed king. He had enough trouble with his wedding list in the first place.

Jesus tells the story in terms of the messianic kingdom. First the friends are invited to the feast. They abuse and kill the messenger/evangelists. Then the Gospel is preached to others. But even they will not be perfect. Some of them will refuse to wear the clothes of the way of life, the shining baptismal pledge of seeking justice and love. They will go into the darkness with the others.

Taxes (Mt. 22:15-22)

Touch the wallet and you touch the quick. There are few surer ways to create a controversy than to create dilemmas on money matters. The Shakespearean line in Othello "He who steals my purse, steals trash" (act 3, scene 3) has only a limited application. People may worry about their good name, but they rarely think of their purse as trash. And, aside from the reading of wills, nothing is likely to stir more passion than discussion about taxes.

The religious leaders who are opposed to Jesus bring up a tender tax question both to embarrass and to trap him. It is painful enough paying taxes to your legitimate government, worse yet to a hated invader and conqueror. "Is it lawful to pay tax to the emperor, or not?" they ask (verse 17). Christ's famed "Render to Caesar" (verse 21) reply eliminated the pandering to popular will, the incitement to lawbreaking and the potential trap laid for him by the agitators. It also walked the razor's edge in the tension that exists between religious and civic responsibilities. It is neither the state nor the church that deserves undivided allegiance. Both can make legitimate demands and both possess corresponding responsibilities. The tension will not disappear.

They Were Sad, You See (Mt. 22:23-33)

The Sadducees were a group of religious scholars who refused to advocate the growing conviction about the resurrection of the body—prompting the pun in the heading of this paragraph. The riddle they proposed about the wife and the seven husbands, all of whom are brothers, was probably a typical conundrum used in their teachings to show the presumed absurdity of bodily resurrection.

Its source was the Levirate Law that stated if a husband died before his wife bore him a child, his brother could and should become her husband so that a baby could be born and the family name not die out. If resurrection of the body is a fact, where does that leave that six-times-widowed woman? Jesus answers that there will be no marriage in heaven. In heaven people will live like angels.

Love (Mt. 22:34-40)

Such religious debates as those about taxes and resurrection reflected typical learning and studying processes in the rabbinical schools. In the context of this Gospel, these learning styles assume more than an academic significance. They become ominous because the debates, in the case of Christ, set the stage for tragic consequences. They are far from the polite discourse of theologians in brotherly battle to refine the meaning of revelation. In another context they would have been nothing more than gentlemanly skirmishes. Here they are life and death issues.

What is the greatest commandment? If Jesus had attempted to pick from among the ten, he would simply have generated a tiresome debate. Instead, he reaches out to another part of the covenant heritage. His words about love being the greatest commandment are taken from Deuteronomy 6:5 and Leviticus 19:18. He reminds his Jewish brethren about these texts which summarize the greatness of their religious heritage and responsibility. Christians, too, often are surprised to discover that the words for the great commandment are in the Old Testament. They fall prey to the idea that holds that the Jews are for justice and the Christians are for love. Ecumenical dialogue has made it clear that Jews are just as interested in love as Christians are, and Christians ought to show that they are equally as dedicated to justice as their Jewish brethren.

The Messiah Is David's Son (Mt. 22:41-46)

Up to this point, the tricky questions have been put to Jesus. Now he takes the initiative. If the messiah is the son of David, how can David call him Lord? They knew the logical answer. They appreciated the grammar and the syntax, but the meaning would be unthinkable to them. Of course the messiah cannot be Lord. Certainly this Jesus who is acclaimed as messiah by the Palm Sunday demonstration is not Lord.

It was embarrassing enough for them to plead ignorance to Christ's question. It was infuriating for them to think he might believe the messiahship attributed to him. Now he adds to it delusions of divine Lordship! Not only will they no longer enter into debate with him, they also will toughen their resolve to stop him.

Reflection

1. Do I enjoy wedding parties?
2. What are the rituals I can always expect at a wedding reception and dinner?
3. Jesus used a wedding party of his time to describe the kingdom of heaven. Is there something about today's wedding celebrations that remind me of heavenly happiness?
4. How would a couple feel if I not only sent regrets to their wedding invitation, but added some insulting remarks?
5. Do I like to dress up when I go to a wedding? What would people think if I didn't?
6. Would I agree that an offending or offensive guest should be asked to leave the wedding celebration?

7. How do I apply Christ's teaching about rendering to Caesar what is Caesar's and to God what is God's?
8. Sadducees did not believe in the resurrection of the body. Many people today do not believe in it either. How would I share my faith in resurrection with them?
9. Did Jesus make up his love commandments, or did he quote them from the Old Testament?
10. What is the value of lively religious discussion, such as the one Jesus engaged in with the religious leaders?

Prayer

Divine storyteller, you took so many events from daily life to make the kingdom of Heaven come alive in the minds and hearts of your listeners. I could look at weddings and taxes today and see spiritual and moral implications. In general I should look at life and through it to your presence here. With your help I will.

23 Final Attack on Religious Hypocrites

Matthew devotes this entire chapter to Christ's summary argument against the hypocritical religious officials of the day. Not all pharisees were like the ones who come under Christ's fierce accusations. Many of them were good men and sincere of heart. But hypocrisy, which is a traditional human failing, is all the more reprehensible in religious leaders.

Hypocrisy (Mt. 23:1-12)

The phylacteries referred to in verse 5 were cosmetic scrolls, small jewelry pieces inside of which were tiny scrolls of the Torah. The hypocrites wore ostentatiously large ones. The original devotional idea was admirable. Why not wear the inspired words close to one's brain? Perhaps the sentiments would be absorbed in the way that plants imbibe sunlight through osmosis. Unfortunately, this did not happen. The larger the phylactery the less the Torah was interiorized.

Avoid the title *rabbi*. Do not call anyone your father (verses 8-9). Fundamentalist religions have used these texts to criticize traditional religions for using reverential titles. One sometimes gets the impression they are more pleased with the needling of the traditionalists than interested in a slavish adherence to the words of Christ. Nevertheless, they have a point. Christ warns the lovers of titles to beware of insisting on such formalities when the more important reality—teaching and fathering—may be forgotten.

Only the truly humble will be great in the kingdom. The exalted must beware lest they fall. Everyone knows how much lip service is paid to humility, but people are prone to arrogance regardless of their station. "Humility" comes from the Latin word meaning earth. Jesus wants his followers to be earthy. This does not involve being shocking or vulgar, but, rather, down to earth, full of common sense.

The Seven Woes (Mt. 23:13-36)

The "woe passages" are a convincing and sad condemnation of religious hypocrites:

1. They have refused the kingdom and act as barriers to anyone who would try to enter it.

2. Their missionary efforts are energetic. But for what purpose? Just to incorporate other once innocent people into a perverted view of God and religion.

3. People are proverbial swearers. No one can prevent it. It is mainly a quaint aberration, but when mixed into religion it becomes a sickening parody of an otherwise forgivable human failing. The hypocrites swear by the gold of the temple and the gift on the altar, that is, by the superficial wealth of religion and the accidental features of holy matters. If there is to be any swearing at all, it should be by the central matter of the house of God and the altar of worship, indicating that the oath takers are aware of the spiritual value of worship within the awesome home of the Lord and the altar of sacrifice.

4. The woe about mint and herbs and seeds also involves a love affair with accidentals rather than essentials. The love of ritual details should never replace devotion to love, justice and mercy. It is a pity that absorption with minute aspects of religious ritual should blind people to the large issues of seeking a just society.

5. The woe about externalism recognizes that the temptation to be captivated by externals at the expense of the interior life is perennial. Virtually any college sophomore can spot such elemental stupidities in some religious people. When someone makes being clean and tidy the substance of religion, trouble is on the horizon. Christ is not approving slovenly and dirty-shirted people, but simply saying that their appearance may be more a matter of cultural ignorance than of spiritual emptiness. Although unhygienic habits may be deplorable, they are not necessarily a sign of spiritual failing. One

should clean the outside of the cup, but it is foolish if the inside is not clean as well.

6. Looking religious is insufficient. Jesus says that the merely good-looking religious person is simply a nice gravestone that covers a worm-eaten corpse. Being well turned-out is no guarantee of virtue. The person of virtue is strong in will and mind, determined to live by a commitment before God.

7. It is typical of leaders to clothe themselves in the glories of past heroes. Every political candidate likes to lay wreathes at the monuments of such people as Lincoln and thus assume the aura of the hero honored. Just as surely, such leaders swear that they would never have treated Lincoln or anyone like him in any adverse manner. Jesus says that the pharisees who decorate the tombs of prophets would have been the first to throw stones at them in times past. They would just as easily have led the opposition to prophecy in years past as they do in the present.

With almost no reserve, he damns them all to hell, calls their bluff and classifies them with every prophet killer from the time of holy Abel to the time of Zechariah. Far from being the holy types they like to associate themselves with on memorial days, they are filthy serpents, biting and deceptive, unworthy of trust and merit, only to be murdered just as fiercely between the temple and the altar as were the martyrs of the past. They, however, would not be martyrs, but outcasts who deserved such judgment.

Lament Over Jerusalem (Mt. 23:37-39)

Overlooking the city of Jerusalem from the Mount of Olives is the lovely chapel of the weeping Christ. A window behind the altar frames a touching picture of the Holy City. On the front of the altar is a mosaic of a hen and some chicks. The chapel memorializes these three verses (37-39) of Christ shedding tears over his beloved city.

Jesus does not want Jerusalem to come under judgment. He loves the city as much as any patriot loves the major city of his or her land or any pilgrim reveres the holiest city of his or her religion. Jesus wants Jerusalem to be the first bearer of the kingdom. He deeply regrets its refusal and subsequent eligibility for the woes that lie ahead. He is too big a person to indulge in petty remonstrances. His tears are real, his anguish genuine. No mother has loved her children more. But Jesus is helpless in the face of their freedom to throw away the prize of the kingdom. He has done all he can. He can only mourn.

Reflection

1. Rabbis wore phylacteries. Do I wear any religious medals or symbols? Do I wear charms or crystals? Why?
2. Do titles mean a lot to me? What causes people to put so much stock in titles?
3. Do I swear to let off steam? How could I use a religious oath for an evil purpose?
4. What would I think of a poor couple, shabbily dressed, in a middle class congregation?
5. In spite of myself, do I consider well dressed, prosperous parishioners automatically to be people of superior character?
6. Am I surprised by Christ's tough talk in his seven woes? Do I expect him only to discuss love and positive matters?
7. Do I feel patriotic about Washington, D.C.?
8. Does the sight of St. Peter's give me a feeling of Catholic pride?
9. People of Christ's time could not imagine the Temple being destroyed. Is it credible to realize that terrorists could bomb St. Peter's?
10. Am I concerned about being judged by God after my death? What about the Last Judgment at the end of the world?

Prayer

Judge of the living and the dead, you are affectionate enough to mourn over the fate of your beloved Jerusalem. Your sternly cleansed the Temple, but were saddened by its forthcoming demise. Your complex approach rescues me from oversimplifying life and religion. With your vision, I see the difference.

24 The End of Time Is Coming

Just as Christians take pride in the world's great cathedrals — in Canterbury, Notre Dame and St. Peter's Basilica — so did the Jews of Christ's time glow with admiration for the Temple of Jerusalem. Solomon's greatest achievement was its building or, as the Bible puts it, establishing the Name of the Lord.

At first the Hebrews were against building a temple. They had both religious and technical objections. To the devout Israelite, God was never in any fixed place, but marched with his people. The ardent believers feared that fixing a permanent abode for the ark of the covenant would deprive their religion of its power and movement. To them, religion had overtones of a community of faith on the move. Israel would always think of its nomadic days in the desert as an ideal time.

But human beings seek stability as well as movement. This conservative tending in the human heart seeks to mold and shape inner dreams into outward permanent forms. Religious architecture is an enduring sign of this other perennial mood of faith. As a shrine, the temple would illuminate the sense of covenant that God established with David and his successors.

The appearance of the temple was a solid reminder that the divine presence brooded over the city and the nation. It was the God who truly ruled the nation from Mount Zion, God who raised up people to stand before kings, governors and the rich to call them to deal justly with people and uphold a high standard of morality.

The technical objection was to the style of architecture, which at first offended the devout. Building styles of the time reflected what was in fashion in the commercial cities of Tyre and Sidon on the coasts of Phoenicia. Solomon hired Phoenician architects and construction engineers to erect the temple. Many old Jews looked with puzzlement and misgiving at the top of Mount Zion where they saw a temple that appeared too much like the pagan sanctuaries used by the hated Canaanites. It seemed too secular, too profane. But in time they came to accept it. In fact, they grew to glory in it. Several centuries later it was destroyed by invading Babylonians. Then, seventy years later, after the return from exile, it was slowly and patiently rebuilt. But it was a sorry sight compared to what Solomon had wrought. Not until the reign of Herod, the king of Christ's time, was a major improvement made upon it. Under Herod's supervision, it was to all intents and purposes rebuilt in a magnificent restoration, so that it shone with the grandeur worthy of Solomon's intentions.

It looked firm and glorious to Jesus and the apostles in the bright sunshine of Holy Week. Just as Jesus had mourned the fate of the Holy City, he now spoke plainly of the doom that awaited the revered sanctuary: "Do you see all these buildings? I assure you, not one stone will be left on another—it will all be torn down" (verse 2). This would be the same as telling a proud Parisian the tragic news that the splendor of Notre Dame will soon disappear in an atomic holocaust, or informing a Roman that a firebomb will destroy St. Peter's within the next generation.

The stunned apostles walked up the Mount of Olives with Jesus, sat overlooking the temple and the city, and asked, "Tell us when all this will occur?" (verse 3). Christ's answer is like a tale about the end of the world and commentators have seen in his observations a prediction of the end of the old covenant. Preachers throughout history have used the words to describe a final end of everything. Their view usually has prevailed, and awesome paintings, such as Michelangelo's *Last Judgment* on the main wall of the Sistine Chapel, which has been viewed by millions of tourists every year for four centuries, have done little to encourage the more limited meaning of Christ's observations. Verse eight is a real clue to the passage: "These are the early stages of birth pangs."

The early stages are false messiahs, wars and natural catastrophes. The birth pangs mean the end of one era and the beginning of a new one. The old covenant will painfully yield to a new one. It is the end of time for the old and the beginning for the new. This does not, of course, exclude the interpretation of the Lord's words to apply to the ultimate end. The kind of language he uses could apply to some extent to any tumultuous ending and time of judgment and there scarcely can be any doubt that the end of time will be a dramatic moment of judgment.

Scholars note that Jesus is using what they call apocalyptic talk, employing a well-known style of rhetoric for describing galvanic changes in history and culture. In the century prior to Christ, this "fire and brimstone" manner of speaking had become quite common. People were used to it, knew the form, understood the import. Jesus adopts this colorful vocabulary to apply to the changes in covenant. The kingdom is being born. Every mother knows the traumas of giving birth. The cultural traumas will be in terms of wars, disasters, conflicting teachings, black suns, dark moons, careening stars, and the pillars of the skies loosening. With this language he tries to shake loose the listeners from any remaining complacency.

The trumpet shall sound and the world will witness the Second Coming of the Son of Man. The richer meaning of this passage is that the resurrection of Christ at Easter is the beginning of that Second Coming, a spiritual advent that will continue till the final revelation at the end of time. Thus, we live between Christ's First Coming in humility and his Second Coming in Glory, a Coming that has already begun with Easter.

The historical realization of the birth pangs includes the destruction of the temple by Vespasian and the destruction of the city of Jerusalem by the Roman legions in A.D. 70. The period is marked by constant political unrest, last-minute savior types and a pervasive darkness clouding the souls of people who sense they are on the verge of tragedy.

Positively, the birth pangs witness the emergence of the kingdom as a visible community of believers, an identifiable church that will be the herald of the Gospel to all nations. The Acts of Apostles show how the kingdom developed into an orderly and ordered community.

Many of the thoughts in this chapter also have been used by spiritual writers to urge moral awareness. It is always hard to read the signs of the times. In the story of Noah the people ate and drank frivolously right up to the hour of the flood. It could be the same now. Just as we watch for a thief in a crime-ridden neighborhood, just as we stick to our work and do not give up, so should we be earnest about the signs of judgement.

Reflection

1. Christ's Last Judgment sermon is about two ends of time, one the final end of the world and the other. . .?
2. Catastrophe language was a biblical literary form to describe end times. What examples do I find here?
3. Does the fact that atomic bombs could destroy our whole planet many times over make Christ's end of the world talk more credible?
4. During the Black Death in the Middle Ages, one third of the population died. Does this account for frequent artistic representations of the final judgment?
5. Every age claims it has false prophets. Who are today's misleading prophets?
6. What was the "abomination" in the Temple?
7. As the year 2000 approaches, one can expect millenarians to emerge, preaching gloom and doom. Are there signs of such millenarism yet?
8. What Old Testament passage provided Jesus with the image of the Son of Man coming in the clouds?
9. Why are sects that gather on hilltops to await the end on a selected day always doomed to disappointment?
10. What grand purpose does the Last Judgment sermon provide?

Prayer

Lord of the End Time, you fill me with Christian realism. You pull me away from both denial of my own death as well as denial of the end of the world. You beckon me to an eternal life perspective that lifts me out of the everyday and saves me from the entrapment of the present or a fixation with the past. Your stirring words alert me to get ready for the future.

25   Virgins, Talents and Charity

Sensible Virgins (Mt. 25:1-13)

The three stories of this chapter flow from the judgement theme established by the story of the birth pangs that led the kingdom to become the church. Members of the kingdom will have to be like sensible virgins who do not waste the oil for their lamps, energetic people who invest and use their talents, perceptive people who realize that their loving compassion is directed toward the Christ who is served, reverenced and loved in every person.

Marriage practices in Christ's time involved three phases, each of them formal and with its own set of rules. The first was the engagement, basically a contract settled by the fathers of the bride and groom. Once this was concluded, there was a betrothal ceremony, which normally was held at the home of the bride's parents. The bride and groom-to-be declared their intention to marry and, in the presence of witnesses, promised fidelity to each other. Presents were given, a bridal shower was held. This betrothal ceremony had legal, binding force. If the man died following it, the woman was considered a widow. The betrothal contract could not be canceled. If somehow it should be, the event would be considered the same as a divorce.

After a year, the marriage took place. The bridegroom, accompanied by his friends, led the bride down the aisle to his father's house. There the parents on both sides guided the couple to the marriage tent, whether inside or outside the house, for the traditional ceremony.

In the story of the sensible virgins, it is the procession of the groom coming to get the bride that is talked about. Presumably the foolish virgins had somehow neglected to be prepared to light the way back to the groom's house. The rest of the wedding party would not wait. They went on to the marriage feast. The sensible virgins enjoyed the party. The foolish ones were left in the dark. "Then the door was barred" (verse 10).

Wise Christians will always have a supply of grace. They will not suffer from a spiritual energy crisis. The meaning of "wise" here is the same as mature. Developing people know the need to plan ahead for the goal to be achieved. Foolish people, in an arrested state of development, forget the need to plan and so the door is closed to them when the feast begins.

Invest Your Talents (Mt. 25:14-30)

Every investment counselor can appreciate the import of the parable of the wasted or uninvested talent. To put money in a savings account is a dictum of common sense. Yet, just as there are people who keep their money in cigar boxes, there are those who do nothing about their spiritual potential. They never grow and because they are stunted by the perverseness of their own lazy inability to polish their God-given talents which would permit them to shine before men and give glory to God, they miss the possibilities of the kingdom. A wasted life is a wasted talent.

A Modern Parable (Mt. 25:31-46)

Scene: The big city
Time: Just after an urban riot
John Stewart looked at the broken windows of his small laundry. His eyes smarted from the smoke that smudged his newly-painted walls. It was the last straw in a series of misfortunes that had come to him during the past year. His wife Pearl had died from cancer. His five-year-old boy Warren had been buried a month ago after being fatally injured by a car.

What was he to do? He had no idea. He went to see his priest for comfort and advice.

"Why not take a month off and spend it at the Trappists," the priest suggested. "I'll get some parishioners to fix up your store and

I'll watch it for you while you're gone."

So John went to the abbey and heard the chants, smelled the dogwood, paced the paths through the fields and barns, and prayed that the heaviness in his heart would be taken away. One day an old monk said to him: "John, I want you to take this copy of the New Testament home with you. Read it every night for fifteen minutes. I promise you that you will be filled with new hope, joy and lightness of heart very soon."

John took the old man's advice. After he went home, he devoted every evening to reading the gospels and soon found that he possessed an inner peace that he had not known for a long time.

One summer evening he came upon the story of Christ in the house of Simon the Pharisee. John was outraged at the crude way the pharisee received Christ. He smiled as he read how Magdalene came in and gave Jesus the hospitality he had been denied by his host.

To himself, John mused, "If Jesus ever came to my laundry, I would treat him like a king."

"John, I'm coming tomorrow."

The voice startled John. It touched him with challenge and anticipation. The Lord was coming to *his* house.

The next morning John polished the windows and waxed the counter. Everything shone for the King. The local policeman came in, looking distressed. "My wife Lucy left me a week ago," he told John. "I haven't eaten a decent meal since."

"Let me make you some food."

While his friend ate, John discussed his recent problems and the new comfort he was receiving from the gospels.

"John," said the policeman, "you are nourishing both my body and my soul. I am grateful."

Customers came and went. It was mid-afternoon and Christ had yet to appear.

The neighborhood social worker came in carrying a bulging attache case and looking as if she were ready to chuck it all and go find a nice suburban husband. "I'm sick and tired of forms, forms, forms!" she said. "John, how can I ever get to help people if I have to spend half my life making reports and writing everybody up in triplicate?"

"I know what you mean, Eleanor. You know, I have lots of time these days. If you like, I'd be glad to help you. I could contact some of the people. I know a lot of them. Let me see them and fill out the forms and then you can spend time counseling and directing them."

"Your help would mean a lot, John. I wonder what lucky star brought me to you today."

The social worker departed. It moved on toward closing hour of 7 p.m. Still, no Lord. John stared absently out his store window, aching to see his Christ. Instead, he witnessed an attempted purse snatching as a small boy whipped by an old woman and tried to steal her pocketbook. She was, however, a veteran of ghetto life and knew well how to hold on to her purse. With surprising swiftness, she grabbed the boy by the collar and called for the police. John moved quickly out to help her. "Please don't call the police," he pleaded. 'The boy is so small. Come into my store and let's talk about it."

Once they were settled inside, the two adults noticed how poor the boy was. His shirt would not survive another laundering and his shoes had worn down at both heels and soles. The old lady, now calmed, mused, "He looks so much like my grandson." John proposed a bargain. "Let's make a man of this boy. You buy him a new shirt. I'll get him some shoes and we'll give him a small new start." She agreed and the boy and the old lady left together, he munching on an apple.

But no Jesus came.

Sadly, John closed his shop and went to his living room to read the Bible. Tonight, however, he had no heart for it. He closed the book with an impatient hand and decided to watch TV. The first picture that appeared on the screen was that of the policeman, with the contented face of a recently fed man.

"John, it is I."

The next image was that of the social worker, displaying her half-empty attache case. She was catching up on her work.

"John, it is I."

Last came the old lady and the young boy. She still clutched her purse tightly, but her face was soft with affection for the boy throwing out his chest in his new shirt and placing his shoes at an angle to catch the glint of the sun.

"John, it is I."

John's eyes widened with recognition as his heart caught the message of the New Testament: "I assure you, as often as you did it for one of these, you did it for me" (Mt. 25:40).

Reflection

1. Does Christ's judgment talk make me uneasy? Should it?
2. If there were no divine judgment awaiting me, would that make a difference in my behavior?
3. Am I a person who never makes a judgment on the goodness or evil of my behavior, or that of others?
4. Am I like the foolish virgins in that I seek not the "oil" of grace that will light my way to the next life?
5. Do I use and develop my talents and gifts?
6. What happens to a gift that is never used?
7. How often am I aware of Christ's presence in others?
8. Could I see Christ in a person who drives me up the wall?
9. What should I do when Christ comes to me through difficult people?
10. Can I think of a process that will aid me to serve Christ in others?

Prayer

Hidden Christ, you visit me in a variety of persons. I admit I seldom think of seeing you in them. I tend to see you only in the sacraments and other sacred realities. Yet, you approach me every day for food, clothing, caring, and a drink of water. Make me aware. Make me remember.

26 To Die in Jerusalem

Prediction of Passion (Mt. 26:1-2)

Although he is idealistic, Jesus never loses a sense of tough realism. Surrounded by fame and acclaim, called "David" by an admiring people, he apparently would be immune to any move by authorities to touch him. But he senses the real mood of his enemies and predicts, in the face of all odds, that martyrdom awaits him before the week is out. It will happen at the beginning of Passover.

Conspiracy (Mt. 26:3-4)

Even as Jesus is preparing the apostles for the tragedy at Passover, the religious leaders of Jerusalem are meeting to plot his murder. They do not think Passover is a good time for such a move. The momentum of events will, however, overtake all those involved.

Mary Anoints Jesus (Mt. 26:6-13)

Both Matthew and John tell the story of Mary anointing Christ for his forthcoming burial. Matthew places the event in the house of Simon the Leper. John places it in the home of Martha, Mary and Lazarus. The latter seems more likely since Christ's friendship with those three probably would lead him to seek one last moment of comfort before the trials ahead.

The objection about wasting expensive perfume is perennially applied to wasting money on expensive churches and shrines. Jesus says the sweet oil is not wasted. It is a rehearsal for his burial. The outstanding critic of "waste," Judas, left this scene to make more money on a betrayal scheme.

Passover Preparation (Mt. 26:17-19)

Christ sends the apostles to a friend to ask him for a room to celebrate the Passover meal. Jesus speaks of the "appointed time." This use of the word "time" is similar to the axiom which states that the power of an idea whose hour has come is greater than the tread of mighty armies. Jesus knows his hour is at hand and takes firm command of the details that lead toward it.

The Supper Begins (Mt. 26:20-25)

It is Holy Thursday evening. The scene was probably very much as it appears in Da Vinci's *Last Supper*. The evening begins as a joyous occasion — quite similar to Americans sitting down to a Thanksgiving Day dinner. No memory warmed the heart of a believing Jew more than the divine delivery from Egypt at the Exodus. There was no better way to celebrate than to feast with a roast lamb.

Jesus quickly dispels the happiness with the shocking announcement that one of the apostles is a traitor. Think again of Da Vinci's painting, which captures the looks of dismay and astonishment on the faces of the disciples. Eleven of them quite rightly can protest innocence: "Surely, it is not I, Lord?" (verse 25).

The clue about dipping the hand in the dish is ambiguous since everyone had done so. Jesus lets the painful accusation sit in the air without deliberately naming the culprit publicly. But, in an aside, he lets Judas know of his own awareness of the betrayal.

Eucharist (Mt. 26:26-30)

The Passover customs in Christ's time called for slaying the lambs at specified places, then taking a portion of the lamb to the priests at the temple for sacrificial purposes. The remainder of the lamb was taken home for the meal, attended by no fewer than ten men, and no more than twenty.

The menu included bitter herbs to recall the grief of slavery in Egypt, unleavened bread dipped in a sweet sauce to recall the joy of freedom after the liberation and four ritual cups of wine. Normally, the father of the household blessed the first cup and then passed it to all the participants. Following this, the youngest son asked, "Why is this night the most important of all nights?"

The father replied by telling the story of the liberation from Egypt and the institution of the Passover. As the story ended the group sang the rousing Hallel (for Halleluiah, meaning praise; the "iah" is a short form for God):

Praise, you servants of the Lord praise the name of the Lord
Blessed be the name of the Lord both now and forever.
From the rising to the setting of the sun, is the name of the Lord
to be praised.

—Ps. 113:1-3

The next phase of the ritual meal was a thanksgiving for all blessings, especially for the bread. As the meal progressed, a third and fourth cup of wine were blessed and passed around.

On that holy night Jesus took two of the existing ceremonies and gave them a profound new meaning. As we have seen, there were blessings of the four cups of wine and blessing of the bread. The disciples had shared in many a Passover meal and knew what to expect. Since they possessed the reverent conservatism of the deeply religious, they did not anticipate or desire any change in the rites. But Jesus did introduce some changes into the centuries-old ritual. He transformed the old covenant into the new. Taking the unleavened bread, he blessed it, that is, pressed his hands upon it and poured into it his divine vitality. His hands became the transforming fire bringing this bread into the realm of utter holiness. To make sure the observers realized what was happening, he spoke new and startling words:

"Take and eat, this is I — My Body" (verse 26).

And they ate of the Bread of Life.

The second change occurred in the blessing of the third cup of wine (it is not certain which cup of wine was used for the Eucharist).

"Here," he said, "drink of this, for this is My Life — My Blood. . . ."

In case they still did not appreciate what he was saying, he added, ". . . of the new and eternal covenant. This is My Life of the new covenant" (verse 28). In thus blessing the bread and the cup, Jesus established a new paschal meal. When he called this event a

147

new covenant he could count on the apostles understanding him in terms of the popular prophecy of Jeremiah: "Behold, the days are coming when I shall make a new covenant with the house of Israel" (Jeremiah 31:31-40).

Blood seals a covenant. At Mount Sinai, after the giving of the Torah (Ten Commandments), which was the life-giving first covenant, Moses took a basin of lamb's blood, representing God's life, and sprinkled it on the altar and the people. Thus the treaty/covenant between God and the people was sealed in the blood of the lamb. So also the cup of Christ's blood in the Mass seals the covenant of the new dispensation.

At this institution of the Eucharist, Christ begins in earnest his final paschal action. He begins the journey that will take him through the dark waters of death to ultimate glory at his Father's right hand. Jesus identifies himself with the bread and wine and also with the lamb of sacrifice. He will face trial, the way of the Cross, death and burial, before his triumphant resurrection and the sending of the Spirit.

Foretelling Peter's Denial (Mt. 26:31-35)

In the midst of this exaltation and solemnity Jesus introduces the sad comment that the apostles will abandon him and that Peter will deny him. Their faith in him will be shaken. Peter protests that this will not happen and Jesus tells him that before morning he will have denied him. The Last Supper thus begins on a note of betrayal and ends on the theme of apostolic loss of faith.

The Agony in the Garden (Mt. 26:36-46)

The city of Jerusalem rests on Mount Zion. Opposite the city is the Mount of Olives. In the valley between the two hills in the Garden of Gethsemane. It is still there today. Centuries-old olive trees grow there and perhaps some of them were present that evening to witness the agonized prayer of Christ. There is a shrine church near-by whose windows are deep purple so that the interior reflects the tragic mood of Christ on that evening.

Jesus brings the favored three, Peter, James and John, to share the vigil of the Crucifixion. He prays that the cup of imminent humiliation will be taken from him and asks to be spared the Passion. He may well have been thinking of a promise of deliverance made to Isaiah:

See, I am taking from your hand the cup of staggering;
The bowl of my wrath you shall no longer drink.

—Is. 51:22

Clearly, the Father makes no such promise to his Son in this instance. Jesus knows he must take the cup. He turns to his three friends for comfort, seeking some human support in his hour of dread decision. As is so often the case in life, he does not find it. When he most needs his friends, they are asleep. Overcome by the lateness of the hour and the heavy feasting, insensitive to the drama about to unfold, they lapse into indifferent slumber.

Twice more Jesus prays and each time finds his friends asleep. As the classic text puts it, they could not even spend one hour with him, while he wrestled to accept his destiny. Jesus concluded each of his prayers with an openness to the Father's will. His experience is a model for all. His resistance to the call can be shared by anyone faced with painful decisions. His loneliness is typical of anyone called to a momentous decision. His heroic acceptance of the Father's will is an ideal toward which all believers should strive.

The Arrest (Mt. 26:47-56)

The question that most troubles the imagination in the scene of the arrest is why Judas betrayed his friend. There are almost as many theories as there are theoreticians, but all hang the implication that Judas is blind to the real meaning of Jesus. He never could come fully to trust and believe in Christ. His loss of confidence in Jesus may be traced to an excessive preoccupation with money or to a secret desire to be a prominent member of the new, presumably political order that Jesus would establish. The rock opera *Jesus Christ Superstar* implies that Judas thinks of Jesus as momentarily deranged, that it is madness for Jesus to assume messianic and divine pretensions. *Superstar* suggests that this is what motivated Judas. The betrayer then felt the arrest would bring Jesus to his senses, that he would disclaim messiahship and divinity and return to the real world.

Since all human beings possess a complex of motivations, it cannot be said with certainty what blinded Judas. The fact is that he placed a traitorous kiss on the lips of one who always loved him. Jesus even called him friend as he received this gesture of peace.

Judas the traitor and Peter the denier are contrasted in the arrest scene. Peter uses violence to defend Christ. But Jesus will have nothing of violence. If he wanted protection he could have summoned legions of angels to be a palace guard. He puts his trust not in the violent sword but in the nonviolent Cross.

No longer is he the anguished beseecher of Gethsemane. He has resolved to do his Father's will. Angels have comforted him and he is now in command. He was not rushed toward martyrdom. That would be a perverse form of glamorous pride. Instead, he pondered it and agonized over it. But once it was clear that it was the direction in which he must move, he does so with nobility and serenity. So much so that he places a common sense question to his captors: "Am I a brigand that you come armed with swords and clubs to arrest me? From day to day I sat teaching in the temple precincts, yet you never arrested me" (verse 55).

The Trial Begins (Mt. 26:57-68)

The trial opens in the church court. The religious leaders had previously intended to wait until after Passover, but the tide of events seems to have overwhelmed them. They wanted immediate action, so they commissioned Judas to find a quiet place where they could pick up Jesus and bring him secretly to a hearing. They bribed false witnesses to produce some convincing criminal testimony but almost failed until two came forward with a conspiracy charge.

These men perverted Christ's words about destroying the temple in three days to mean that he was planning a guerilla attack on the temple buildings with the intention of vandalizing and destroying the sanctuary. When the judge asked Christ to reply to this accusation, he could have explained the spiritual interpretation about resurrection that he intended by the statement. He had been referring to the temple of his body, though he also foresaw that invading armies would one day actually destroy the Jerusalem sanctuary. But Jesus kept silent because he knew neither answer would make any sense to them. Resurrection was unthinkable even though they believed in the possibility. And, given the cozy relations with Rome, it scarcely seemed likely that any Roman army would launch an attack on the temple in the foreseeable future. To them, either answer would be avoiding the issue and an implicit cover-up of his supposed real intention, to lead a terrorist incursion on the temple area.

The judge then moved to the issue of blasphemy. Followers of Christ had acclaimed him messiah and Son of God. "I order you to tell us under oath before the living God whether you are the messiah, the Son of God" (verse 63). Jesus replies, "It is you who say it" (verse 64). In other words, he asserts his messiahship and divinity and goes on to include his future glorification and right to be judge of all those who have refused to accept his grace and salvation.

Caiphas, the judge, may not fully appreciate what Jesus is saying, but he has enough evidence in these words to affirm what seems to him and the court to be blasphemy. The tearing of the robes was a typical gesture of outrage. He asks the court for a verdict.

"He deserves death" (verse 66).

This is not a sentence, for the church court is not competent to give the death sentence. That was the role of the civil court to which they would take Jesus at dawn on Good Friday (Matthew 27:1-2). They turned on Christ, hit him in the face and spit on him, tormenting him with curses.

Peter's Denial (Mt. 26:69-75)

There is an old saying about keeping your words short and sweet for you may have to eat them some day. Peter had been loud and voluble in avowing his loyalty to Christ. But, when the chips were down, he was a coward. While Jesus went through the first phase of his trial, Peter was nearby, not as a supporter but as a curious bystander. Several people recognized him and identified him as a friend of Jesus. Three times Peter denied his association with Christ, concluding his last denial with cursing and swearing. And the cock crowed. Properly filled with shame and remorse, "he went out and wept bitterly" (verse 75).

Reflection

1. Am I a realist? Am I a romantic? A dreamer?
2. The Last Supper had several symbolic foods. We have symbolic foods also: turkey, cranberries, champagne, birthday cakes, apples. What are some others?
3. The Last Supper also had rituals: wine toasts, songs, storytelling, dialogue and readings from Scripture. What are some of our meal rituals?
4. The first Eucharist occurs at a friendship paschal meal. Is that why we speak of our altar as a table? Does this account for the importance of community at Mass?
5. The first Eucharist contains the words of institution that turn bread and wine into the body and blood of Christ? How does this connect with Good Friday?
6. Why do we call the Eucharistic table the altar of sacrifice?
7. The bread is broken. Christ's body is broken. Will I also be broken with Christ?
8. The cup of Christ's blood is poured out. Will I also be poured out with Christ?
9. Have I been a Judas/betrayer and a Peter/denier at times?
10. Jesus wanted and needed a support group at Gethsemane. Am I present to support Jesus today present in the distressed, the needy and the oppressed?

Prayer

My Redeemer, the powerful narrative of your passion and death always moves me deeply. Your graciousness at the Last Supper offers me the extraordinary treasure of the Eucharist. Only with you can I walk the way of the Cross. Only in you will I be broken and poured out — and thus transformed.

27 No Greater Love

The Suicide of Judas (Mt. 27:3-10)

The condemnation of Christ revealed to Judas his tragic mistake. He returned the thirty pieces of silver to the conspirators and confessed his sin. They offered him no comfort, just a cynical indifference to his foolishness in being their patsy. Subversion is hardly a citadel of integrity.

The fatal flaw in Judas' character, namely, his inability to trust and believe in another, now leads him to self-destruction. While he had the decency to acknowledge the innocence of Jesus, he lacked the sublimity of faith that would have rescued him from the despair that drove him to suicide. He never appreciated the offer of forgiveness that was central to the mission of Jesus. Christ would be nailed to the tree of hope. Judas died on the tree of despair.

The conspirators possessed a sufficient trace of honor not to put the money into the temple treasury. Instead, they used it to buy a plot of land to be used as a cemetery for foreigners.

The Civil Trial (Mt. 27:11-26)

The veteran Roman soldier, Pontius Pilate, became a master of compromise when he was appointed governor of Judea in A.D. 26. His skills at controlling this trouble spot for the interests of the empire kept him in power there for ten and one-half years. His experience with the trial of Jesus was preceded by two other potentially explosive incidents.

Shortly after Pilate arrived in Judea a detachment of his reserve troops marched into Jerusalem flaunting bronze images of Emperor Tiberius on their regimental standards. They should have known this would be a provocation to a people whose religious beliefs recoiled from images, whether engraved, sculpted or painted. "You shall not carve idols for yourselves in the shape of anything in the sky above or on the earth below or in the waters beneath the earth" (Ex. 20:4). The people conducted a five day mass protest demonstration in Jerusalem at the end of which Pilate ordered the offensive standards removed.

Sometime later, Pilate constructed an aqueduct to bring water into Jerusalem from a water supply near Bethlehem. He paid for it with funds from the temple treasury. This news incited another riot, which he suppressed with bloodshed. Theoretically, there was no religious reason for this outbreak since a tradition of Jewish law allowed for the use of temple money for public works. In addition, Pilate probably received the cooperation of temple officials to obtain the money since he did not plunder the funds by sacrilegious entry into the temple area. Whatever the actual reason was for the violence, Pilate was persuaded to move gingerly with this touchy people.

It is therefore easy to see why he was so cautious when the officials brought Jesus to him for trial. He asks Christ if he is a king. It is not clear why he would place this question to Jesus since this was not the substance of the charge from the church court. Possibly he assumed from reports about the Palm Sunday incident that Jesus had some revolutionary dream based on kinship with the family of David.

Jesus agrees that he is a king but does not bother to explain that he has no political intentions. In John's Gospel he does expand on the spiritual nature of his kingship and Pilate shows no ability to understand this avowal.

The accusers of Jesus then made a series of unspecified charges. Pilate gave Jesus a chance to defend himself, but he remained silent. This annoyed Pilate for several reasons. For one thing, he did not want any new uprisings like the two he previously dealt with. He also sensed that Jesus was innocent. Why, then, was he letting the tide of events turn against Jesus?

Beyond these two factors, Pilate came to the conclusion that jealousy was the main objection of the religious officials. As a way out of the dilemma he decided to link the Passover amnesty privilege to this case. He knew the people's choice this year was Barabbas, a convicted robber and revolutionary who had a romantic appeal for the people because he symbolized their aggressive hatred of the Roman occupation forces.

Pilate also was aware of the popular ovation Jesus had received on Palm Sunday. He counted on this to obtain the freedom of Christ. The people had the unexpected choice of two popular candidates for amnesty. On the face of things, Jesus would be the logical choice.

While they deliberated, Pilate received a message from his wife warning him to leave Jesus alone: "Do not interfere in the case of that holy man. I had a dream about him today which greatly upset me" (verse 19).

Meanwhile, the religious officials convinced the crowd to pick Barabbas and call for Christ's execution. Several things regarding the size of the mob should be kept in mind while pondering this scene. The vast throngs usually pictured in movies and paintings are misleading. Most likely the group was comparatively small, a few hundred at the very most. For one thing, it was dawn. Not too many people would be up yet. Secondly, very few would even know about the arrest and the swift succession of religious and civil trials. Thirdly, the narrow street in front of Pilate's palace would hardly contain the ungainly mobs normally seen in grandiose biblical epics. And, finally, the crowd that actually did gather was probably a picked group of like-minded people quickly assembled by the religious officials to back up their plans. It is never too difficult to convene a loyalist faction.

Jesus never attempted to organize his followers and most of those who admired and loved him were among the helpless and powerless. It is not surprising therefore that they came to his defense neither on that morning nor in the nine fateful hours that remained of his life. If nothing else, the sheer speed of events precluded it.

Thus, when Pilate asked for their verdict, the packed jury called for the release of Barabbas and the death sentence for Jesus. Pilate was not satisfied with their bloodthirsty yells for crucifixion. He tried to reason and argue with them. He asked them to name the crime. They screamed back a relentless chant, "Crucify him!"

Pilate had seen enough violence and riots in his tenure and he was in no mood to cope with a full-scale police action in a city filled with religious pilgrims on the eve of the holiest day of the liturgical year. For all his pragmatism, he possessed a hint of conscience. He knew Jesus was innocent. But he separated his legal from his moral conscience. Legally, he felt bound to issue the death sentence. Morally, he tried to absolve himself by the famed hand washing. "I am innocent of the blood of this just man. The responsibility is yours" (verse 24).

The distinction is of course academic in this case. A morally courageous man would not have yielded to mob pressure and then debased the situation by what history can only regard as a cheap gesture to avoid an exercise of justice. In any other case this remote provincial governor would have been forgotten. Pilate's deed is forever remembered in the Apostle's Creed. Jesus "suffered under Pontius Pilate."

Matthew notes that the crowd yelled, "His blood be upon us and upon our people" (verse 25). That phrase has unfortunately been misapplied throughout Christian history to mean that all Jews were and are responsible for the death of Christ. Many a Christian preacher accused Jews of all times of being guilty of deicide.

Worse yet, this view gave justification to Christian pogroms against Jews such as those that happened during the Crusades, the Inquisition and 19th century Czarist Russia. It justified anti-semitism. In recent years both Christian scholars and official Christian positions have repudiated this wrong interpretation of the passage. Vatican Council II's Declaration on the Jews expressly disavows any imputation to the Jewish community living or dead for the execution of Christ. There is no divine curse on all Jews due to the involvement of a few of them in the trial scene before Pilate.

The legal and moral responsibility for Christ's death lay with Pilate and the pressure group that pushed him in that trial scene at dawn so many centuries ago. The extravagant statement about wanting his blood and letting responsibility for it rest on the people is the rhetorical cry of a mob and not a self-inflicted curse on all Jews which God presumably is only too glad to implement through Christian terrorism.

Once the sentence was given, the usual brutal processes of capital punishment were set in motion. Step one was the scourging, a brutal flogging with a leather whip that had ankle bones of sheep at the tips of the thongs. This was a routine beating meant to weaken the victim so that he died as quickly as possible as a result of the shock and blood loss.

The Crowning With Thorns (Mt. 27:27-31)

Jesus is now in the hands of professional executioners. To their usual brutalities they add a bizarre detail: the crowning with thorns, a humiliating mockery of Christ's alleged kingship. Few scenes in all of history so move the hearts of believers to pity and compassion for Jesus as does this cruel debasing of the kindest and most loving man the world has ever seen. In his music for the Matthew Passion, Bach reflects a mystical effort to move to the heart of this moment.

O Sacred Head surrounded
By crown of piercing thorn
O bleeding Head so wounded
Reviled and put to scorn
Death's pallid hue comes o'er thee
The glow of life decays
Yet angel hosts adore thee
And tremble as they gaze.

The Way of the Cross (Mt. 27:32-34)

The place of execution was outside the city walls. The soldiers placed the cross-beam on Jesus's shoulders. The scenes and meditations from the Stations of the Cross serve as well as any commentary on these lines. Jesus is brought to Golgotha, the Skull Place. He is offered a potion to dull his pain. He tastes it but refuses to drink it.

The Crucifixion (Mt. 27:35-44)

Meditations on the crucifixion of Jesus, especially from the Middle Ages onward have tended to consider the physical sufferings of Jesus. The bodily pain of the Lord has helped millions to accept their own suffering in a redemptive manner. Our own times are shifting to the psychological appreciation of the passion. The imminent approach of death is faced in a series of stages.

Denial. Death cannot happen to me. Or at least it should not. Or, let it come later. Christ's agony in the garden is an illustration of this very human form of denial. "Let this cup pass from me" (Mt. 26:39).

Bargaining. Again, the Gethsemane scene shows Christ using delaying tactics, stalling for time as anyone does when faced with the prospect of death. Over and over he prays for the cup to pass. He has more work to do, more good to perform. More time, please.

Sadness. "My heart is ready to break with grief" (Mt. 26:38). Christ's sorrow and sadness are caused by so many things. The unfinished business. The extra help his apostles still need. One more year of training for them. A further chance to heal and preach. But no. It is all over. Earth's work is done.

Anger. "My God, my God, why have you forsaken me?" (verse 46). The anger of helplessness at the inevitability of the final hour, the sense of abandonment which every terminal patient can testify to — they are here in Christ's outburst to his Father.

Acceptance. In Matthew's account, Christ's final expression is a deep sigh. Luke says the Lord's final expression is "Father into your hands I commit my spirit" (Luke 23:46). At Gethsemane he said he wanted to do the Father's will. Here he surrenders himself to the Father in peace and acceptance.

The Death of Jesus (Mt. 27:45-56)

From noon onward, a strange darkness covered the earth and lent a cloak of mourning to the scene. The outer darkness echoed the inner desolation of Jesus, who cries out, "Eli, Eli lama sabacthani?" (verse 46)—My God, My God, why have you forsaken me? Such an inconsolable cry reveals how closely Jesus identifies with the absolute desolation that sin and death cause in the world.

In a certain sense, it may be said that this cry of Jesus reveals that God for the first time truly realizes what it is like for a man to die. From the incarnation onward God stood within the consciousness of Jesus, realizing the full plight of the human condition, some of it full of pain. Christ's cry of abandonment echoes in the halls of divine awareness, pleading for the enduring, comforting presence that divinity alone can give.

Cruelly, the external listeners misunderstand the words of Jesus. They think he is asking for the reincarnation of Elijah to come and save him. But the internal listener, the Father, does hear. In Matthew this is not so clear. He says Jesus lets out one last death cry and releases his spirit. It is in Luke and John that the richer endings are described. In Luke, Jesus commends his spirit to the Father. He moves into the emptiness of death knowing that his agonized question of abandonment has been heard. Divinity calls him into death with assurance and hope.

In John, Jesus concludes with the priestly prayer "It is finished" (Jn. 19:30). At 3 p.m. in the temple, the High Priest concludes the offering of the Passover lambs with the ritual prayer of completion. Simultaneously, on Calvary, Jesus the Eternal High Priest, the true Lamb of God, speaks his words of sacred completion and goes in peace toward his Father.

At the same moment the veil of the temple was torn in half. The temple building had three rooms, the innermost which originally contained the Ark of the Covenant, upon which dwelt the *Shekinah*, the cloud/glory presence of God. Exodus tells about the veil that shielded this room of the Ark: "You shall make a veil woven of violet, purple and scarlet yarn, and of fine linen twined, with cherubim embroidered on it. It is to be hung on four gold plated columns of acacia wood, which shall have hooks of gold and shall rest on four silver pedestals. Hang the veil from clasps. The ark of the commandments you shall bring inside, behind this veil which hides the holy place from the holy of holies. Set the ark in the holy of holies" (Ex. 26:31-34).

Since the Ark disappeared during the exile, it was not in this rebuilt temple. Instead there was an altar of sacrifice. St. Paul sees in the tearing of the veil the symbolic entrance of Jesus into the eternal sanctuary and the possibility of all sinners having direct access to the grace and mercy of God.

"Like a sure and firm anchor, hope extends beyond the veil through which Jesus, our forerunner, has entered on our behalf, being made high priest forever according to the order of Melchisedech" (Heb. 6:19). "Brothers, since the blood of Jesus assures our entrance into the sanctuary by the new and living path he has opened for us through the veil . . . let us draw near in utter sincerity" (Heb. 10:19-39).

Matthew goes on to record that the earth quaked and numerous bodies of the saints arose and appeared to many. This prelude to Easter symbolized the union of the prophets, martyrs and holy ones of the first covenant with Jesus, the fulfiller of the second. These were the dead spoken of by Paul: "But now Christ has been raised from the dead, the first fruits of those who have fallen asleep" (I Cor. 15:20).

The obvious heroism of Christ and the ensuing marvels moved the centurion in charge of the execution to announce what would become the substance of Christian proclamation: "Clearly this was the Son of God!" (verse 54).

In a Passion story filled with so much betrayal, hostility, cowardice, and abandonment, it is a relief to read that some remained faithful to the end. John's Gospel reminds us that Mary associates herself quietly and strongly with the sufferings of her son and that the apostle John proved his living devotion. Matthew indicates that a group of women, including some relatives, stayed close to Jesus throughout the whole harrowing experience and were prepared to comfort Mary and take care of the details of the burial.

The Burial (Mt. 27:57-61)

Hebrew law required that burial take place within twenty-four hours. This was a health precaution, especially for semi-tropical climates. Stories of prompt burials are told of Sarah in Genesis 23, and Rachel in Genesis 35. Normally, coffins were not used. The bodies were placed either in peon graves covered with stones to prevent access by wolves or jackals or in caves. Many such caves have been discovered near Mount Carmel, where bodies of men and women can be seen either lying on their backs or in hunched positions with their knees under their chins.

In Christ's time the customs called for washing the body and treating it with perfumes and spices. It was wrapped in linen and a linen cloth was placed over the face. Professional wailers frequently were hired. Many of them were blind people who sought the job as a form of regular employment. Egyptians left gifts of food with the body. Jews did not.

Hillsides were favorite places for burial since that is where natural caves could be found for use as burial chambers. The burial cave owned by Joseph of Arimathea was on a small hillside very close to Calvary. (So close in fact, that if the traditional site preserved in the Jerusalem Church of the Martyrdom and Resurrection of Jesus is the actual one, it was little more than a hundred feet away.) A heavy stone was rolled against the cave's opening. Mary Magdalene and Mary the mother of James and Joseph remained there for a time keeping vigil.

The Guards (Mt. 27:62-66)

The religious officials who rejected the idea that Christ's words concerning the destruction of the temple referred to a resurrection now seem very interested in them. They probably do not believe in the possible resurrection of Jesus, but they must worry that the apostles will steal the body and proclaim a false resurrection. They therefore insist that Pilate appoint a guard to stand at the tomb until three days have passed. Pilate gives them permission to guard the tomb. It is not clear whether temple or Roman personnel were used.

And so the vigil begins with the devout women and ends with the unbelieving guard. A mysterious expectation waits in human consciousness. It is a time of meditation. In "The Biography," Merton contemplated the Passion in these words:

And yet with every wound You robbed me of a crime
And as each blow was paid with Blood,
You paid me also each great sin with greater graces.
For even as I killed you,
You made Yourself a greater thief than any in Your company,
Stealing my sins into Your dying life.
Where, on what cross my agony will come
I do not ask You:
For it is written and accomplished here,

On every Crucifix, on every altar.
It is my narrative that drowns and is forgotten
In Your five open Jordans,
Your voice that cries my: "Consummatum est."

—Thomas Merton

Reflection

1. What made Pilate cautious toward the religious leaders when he was dealing with Jesus?
2. The mob before Pilate's house was relatively small. What verifies this?
3. Why is it a mistake to take the words of the mob about Christ's blood being upon them and their people not be used for anti-semitic propaganda? (Anti-semitism should be proscribed anyway.)
4. What spiritual lessons do I draw from the crowning with thorns?
5. The five stages of dying outline the common experiences of dying. What do they tell me about my own attitude toward death?
6. In the cry of abandonment, Jesus experiences the absence of God's presence. Do I lose the divine presence myself from time to time?
7. How would I explain the piercing of the veil of the Temple?
8. What do I make of the darkened sky, earthquakes and resurrections that occur at Jesus' death?
9. Does my meditation on Christ's passion and death help me face the mystery of suffering with more faith?
10. Have I learned to unite my own sorrows with those of Christ for the world's salvation?

Prayer

My Crucified Lord, your Cross saves me from all that oppresses me, above all from sin. Thank you for the best of love, the kind in which you lay down your life for your friends. I adore you O Christ and I praise you, for by your holy Cross you have saved the world.

28 Arise My Love

The luminous story of Easter brings to an end Matthew's account of the founding of the Kingdom by Jesus. Miracles, parables, dialogues, battles, warnings, encouragements, heights of ecstasy such as the Transfiguration, depths of agony such as Gethsemane, prophecies both dark and light and the Way of the Cross all coalesce into the great manifestation of the Kingdom at Easter in the risen body of Christ.

This is the Passover of Christ shining forever. It calls for embraces of joy and the singing of alleluias. The traditional greeting of Christians of the Eastern Churches surges with "Christ is risen, alleluia! He is risen indeed, alleluia!"

Jesus leaves the tomb as from a bridal chamber and fills the two women with joy, telling them to bring the happy news to the eleven.

The two women become the very first heralds of the Good Tidings. It is imagined that they would say to the eleven, to Zion, to the whole world: "Take from us the joyous announcement of the resurrection of Christ. Jesus has left the tomb as fair as a bridegroom."

The Discovery at the Tomb (Mt. 28:1-10)

On the morning of the third day the two Marys returned to the tomb for the last anointings of the body of Jesus. Upon their arrival there is an earthquake. An angel appears like a flash of lightning and moves aside the stone covering the burial chamber. Clothed in a garment as dazzling as bright snow, he tells the women about the Resurrection of Jesus. Then he shows them the empty tomb and instructs them to tell the eleven about Christ's rising. Christ will meet them in Galilee.

In Matthew's Gospel the eternal Galilean makes his last appearance in that land where the first excitement and joy of the Gospel was experienced:

Land of Zebulun, land of Naphtali along the sea beyond the Jordan, heathen Galilee:
A people living in darkness has seen a great light.
On those who inhabit a land overshadowed by death, light has risen.

—Mt. 4:15-16

The light of the historical Christ first shone in Galilee. Now, the light of the Easter Christ will first appear in Galilee. The other Gospel writers will tell of Christ's appearances in Jerusalem. Matthew is content to dwell on the Galilean manifestation.

As the women, filled with joy and awe, make their way back to tell the apostles, they are brought up short by the sudden appearance of Jesus. Overcome by a religious experience beyond words, they pay homage to Jesus and embrace his feet. Jesus speaks to them the age old greeting of Hebrew hospitality, *Shalom*. This greeting of peace is meant to be more than a ritual hello; it is a combination of assurance and the intention to produce an inner confidence and acceptance. In dispelling their anxiety, Jesus causes the first fruits of the redemption, the bringing near of God and people in the most loving of unions.

Jesus dispels their fear. God is not one who enjoys relationships based on terror or intimidation. That is a slave-master transaction. In his presence there is no need to keep up defenses against threat. He is an absolute lover who desires and creates the best in all people. He repeats the instruction about the meeting in Galilee.

The Bribing of the Guard (Mt. 28:11-15)

Matthew alone tells the story of the bribing of the guard as a strengthening of evidence for the empty tomb. The guards were witnesses of the marvels at the grave and reported truthfully all that happened. The religious officials could not shake them in their story so they paid them to keep quiet about the real occurrences and instead to tell a tale about grave robbery. They are told to say they fell asleep briefly and unfortunately, during which time the apostles stole the body of Christ.

The guards objected that they would get in trouble with Pilate.

The officials assured them that they would see to it that Pilate left them alone. Normally, Pilate would not have tolerated a breach of discipline in his troops; but, because of the sensitivity of this situation and the special involvement of the chief religious leaders in Jerusalem, he would most likely overlook the matter in this case. He already washed his hands of Jesus, so he probably would not want to reopen the case. The soldiers pocketed the money and circulated the story that remained the local unbelievers' view of Easter.

Teach All Nations (Mt. 28:16-20)

In his Christmas story, Matthew pointed out that Jesus was of the royal family of David. Then the wise men came and honored the infant as a newly-born king. Now, risen from the dead, Jesus announces that he is king of heaven and earth. To him is given complete authority over all.

This authority grew more obvious during the Gospel story. Jesus has authority to forgive sins, authority to act as the final judge of people and to determine the destiny of his own life. Now, he summarizes again the extent of his kingship: "Full authority has been given to me both in heaven and on earth" (verse 18). Had he listened to the Tempter in the desert, he would have been made a mere earthly emperor (Matthew 4:9). But, remaining obedient to the Father, he faced the demands of life and the cruelties of the Passion and Death and thus receives a cosmic Lordship.

Jesus now commands the apostles to go forth and teach all nations. This is the commission to evangelize the world, to call people from sin to grace, from evil to union with Christ. It is a mandate to bring all people to a living, conscious and active faith. It will involve baptism into the faith through the Father, Son and Holy Spirit.

It will take a while before the eleven understand the full impact of Christ's words. They will need all the experiences that Luke outlines so well in the Acts of the Apostles.

The Holy Spirit will come fifty days hence at Pentecost to spark the first flowering of their resolve. They gradually will move away from Jerusalem, up to Antioch. Then, through the dynamic leadership of Paul, the Gospel will flow out to the ends of the earth.

As the eleven gaze on Jesus they may well have understood the theme of the Song of Songs, "Arise, my love." Jesus, the beloved of the Father, has indeed risen. He commands them to evangelize the world, to tell everyone about the boundless love of God. The works of God are not something of the past, but something living and active in every corner of the earth.

Their witness as Christian missionaries will be paschal events showing forth the death and resurrection of Jesus. They are the heralds of the kingdom, the dynamic spiritual aspect of the church. They will proceed to organize a church, but they will never forget its Kingdom nature, its spiritual essence.

They went on to speak a language that was relevant to their world. They spoke the message of the first century in first century terms and thus affected the lives and decisions of the people of their day. That enduring message needs the language and spirit of each new age to become persuasive and compelling. Today's missionaries must not dwell on the first century message. That would be collecting antiques. The message must be taken and retranslated in contemporary terms.

It must address itself to the existence of people enchanted by three hours of prime-time TV every night, rattled by hours of freeway commuter traffic, shaken by financial crises and wars, afflicted with headaches, tensions, marriage problems, rebellious youth, cranky relatives, cancers, heart attacks, low sugar levels — and spiritual emptiness.

Angels hum in the springtime glory of Christ's Easter. Their song blurs when witnesses of the Kingdom fail to carry on the mission mandated on that Galilean hill: Go out! Be my witnesses. Fearlessly bring the message of my wondrous deeds, my paschal work!

Too many chains bind people today, chains of anxiety, fear and death. But Christ broke these chains. He burst the bonds of death and brought us freedom.

Every year, the freedom of Easter takes on the bright sound of a trumpet blast, for people in Christ are truly free. The man in Christ is the master of everything because he serves the possessor of everything and is possessed by Christ himself. Paul said it best: "All things are yours, whether it be the world, or life or death, or the present or the future: all these are yours, and you are Christ's, and Christ is God's" (I Cor. 3:22-23).

He is risen indeed. Alleluia!

Inherit the Kingdom prepared for you from the creation of the world .

—Mt. 25:34

Reflection

1. How do images like the sunrise, a butterfly and the birth of a child symbolize Easter for me?
2. Do I have other favorite symbols?
3. Christ's first Easter word to the women is "shalom-Peace." Does our Lord's peace still the restlessness of my heart?
4. Have I thought much about my immortality?
5. Jesus dispels the fear of the women and replaces it with love. Have I learned that love lets go of fear?
6. Do I realize that by my baptism, Christ calls me to share my faith with others?
7. Jesus wants all members of the church to be evangelizers. What do I expect of my evangelizing community?
8. Do the evangelizers I know use the hard sell or an invitational approach? Which style do I favor?
9. What events in a person's life incline them to conversion?
10. What is the happiest Easter I can remember? What made it so?

Prayer

Risen Jesus, you fill me with hope and songs of alleluias. You convince me there is a future full of promise. You have conquered the world's worst evils — sin and death. I praise and thank you with all my heart. Alleluia! Amen!

12 Silver

Thunderbird Point
Enter
left
Thunderbird Right
Jegonis left
End park & look
    down in hole !

lawnchairs